G000153584

hotels • restaurants • spas • wineries • lodges

newzealandchic

For regular updates on our special offers, register at

www.thechiccollection.com

hotels • restaurants • spas • wineries • lodges

newzealandchic

text nicky adams • annette tan • kerry o'neill • elena nichols

thechiccollection

publisher'sacknowledgements

Welcome to *New Zealand Chic*, the 14th book in The Chic Collection that we started in 2003 to present 'wow' destinations to the independent-minded traveller seeking affordable luxury and different experiences.

Creating *New Zealand Chic* gave us the opportunity to discover a country of immense natural beauty and variety infused with an amazing spirit of purpose and optimism. It is also a country that promises joy and abundant memories in the pursuit of its discovery.

Projects of this magnitude require a great collective effort and I would particularly like to single out the following parties. Firstly, James Mcleod, who spent four weeks travelling around both islands, and many other sleepless nights on the phone making sure that this book came together. Thanks are also due to Air New Zealand and the New Zealand Tourism Board in London, Neil Pollett of New Zealand Luxury, Karine Thomas of Navigate Oceania, Wendy Dobson of Art of Travel, Katy Lamb of Turquoise Holidays, Mike Laven of The Peppers Martinborough Hotel, Richard Riddiford of Palliser Estate Wines, Ross George of Direct Capital Partners and Michael Kelly of Lodge at 199. Last but not least, the 'night shift' team at Editions Didier Millet who once again pulled out all the stops, around the clock.

I hope that this book will be a great inspiration to guide you on your way through the many sites and experiences on offer in this beautiful unspoilt country. Go now, or sooner!

Nigel Bolding
publisher

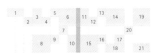

COVER CAPTIONS:

1: The Cavalli Beach House Retreat.
2: Golf course in front of Millbrook.
3: Skiing down the Remarkables.
4: Green-lipped mussels.
5: The Burbury Suite at Sherwood Lodge.
6: A meal out in the vineyard.
7: Contemporary Maori art pieces.
8: Outdoors, Accolades Boutique Hotel.
9: Riding the Shotover Jet at Queenstown.
10: The Castle Matakana.
11: Split Apple Rock.
12: Fashion wear from Karen Walker.
13: A cluster of starfish.
14: The volcanic cone of Mount Ruapehu.
15: Riverview Vineyard in Hawke's Bay.
16: The Lighthouse Suite at The Boatshed.
17: Yacht in a sailing competition.
18: dine by Peter Gordon, at SKYCITY Grand Hotel.
19: The Tree Houses at Hapuku Lodge.
20: Manhattan-style urban living at Hotel Off The Square.
21: Lakeside dining at Huka Lodge.

PAGE 2: *Family outing by the seaside.*

THIS PAGE: *Relaxing in a hammock.*

OPPOSITE: *Picnic on the beach.*

PAGE 6: *Paragliding.*

PAGES 8 AND 9: *The colours on a parachute.*

executive editor
melisa teo

editor
gregory lee

assistant editor
siti sarah supri

designers
lisa damayanti • felicia wong

production manager
sin kam cheong

first published in 2007 by
bolding books
49 wodeland avenue,
guildford gu2 4jz, united kingdom
enquiries : nigel@thechiccollection.com
website : www.thechiccollection.com

designed and produced by
editions didier millet pte ltd
121 telok ayer street, #03-01
singapore 068590
telephone : +65.6324 9260
facsimile : +65.6324 9261
enquiries : edm@edmbooks.com.sg
website : www.edmbooks.com

©2007 bolding books
design and layout © editions didier millet pte ltd

Printed in Singapore.

All rights reserved. No part of this publication may be reproduced, stored in a retrieval system, or transmitted in any form or by any means, electronic, electrostatic, magnetic tape, mechanical, photocopying, recording or otherwise, without prior written permission from the publisher.

isbn: 978-981-4155-89-2

contents

newzealandbyregion

newzealandbychapter

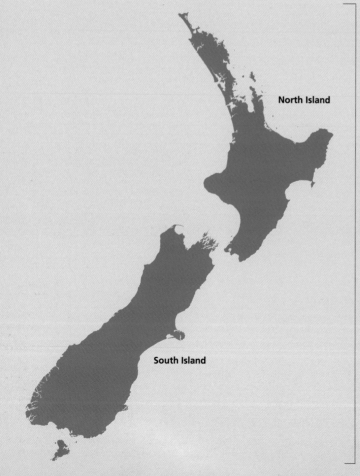

North Island

Food + Wine

South Island

introduction

In the South Pacific Ocean 1,600 km (1,000 miles) from the nearest landmass of east Australia, is New Zealand. Only about 800 km (500 miles) from the International Date Line, it claims to be the first country in the world to see the sun rise. Comparable in size to the British Isles, the country is made up of two large islands (North Island and South Island) and a number of much smaller ones around the periphery. The North and South Islands are separated by the Cook Strait, which is 20 km (12 miles) wide at its narrowest point, and both islands are distinctly different.

The South Island contains the largest land mass in New Zealand, and is characterised by its number of mountains—18 peaks that are over 3,000 m (9,800 ft) in height lie along the Southern Alps. The North Island is, however, less mountainous, but marked by volcanic activities.

rocky beginnings

New Zealand is considered to be somewhat of a geographical seedling; its landmass and form were only shaped less than 10,000 years ago. A remnant of the super continent of Gondwanaland, which once consisted of Australia, Antarctica, India, Africa and South America, the country was formed during eons of colliding and shifting of the earth's plate. Eventually breaking off from the last of its neighbouring land masses—Australia and Antarctica—New Zealand still continued to evolve due to seismic activity. Geologically, the North and South Islands are poles apart after being divided by a fault. The result is a display of landscapes so diverse that one would expect to see them spread across an entire continent instead of being concentrated to an archipelago of islands. Snow-topped mountain ranges, glaciers, vast lakes, sand dunes and volcanic peaks are but some of the many spectacular natural sights to behold.

New Zealand's history is interspersed with volcanic activity, and it is fair to assume this will continue to be the case. This is not necessarily a bad thing, as the volcanic rocks give rise to fertile soil, which in turn benefits the dairy, horticulture and wine industries.

THIS PAGE: Snow-capped mountains make up the Southern Alps in the South Island.
OPPOSITE: The intricate details on the roof-top of a Maori meeting house. Also known as mareas, these places served both religious and social purposes in ancient Polynesian societies.

earth, wind and fire

Volcanic activity has been an overriding feature of the history of the North Island—its most spectacular eruption took place 1,800 years ago, forming Lake Taupo as a result. This eruption is recognised to have been the world's most violent volcano eruption in the last 5,000 years. Near to Rotorua on the shores of Lake Tarawera lies the famous Buried Village of Te Wairoa. This 19th-century Maori village was devastated by the unexpected eruption of Mount Tarawera; its famous Pink and White Terraces were totally erased. In recent times, an earthquake in 1931 wrecked the Hawke's Bay region. The city of Napier was destroyed, with effects also felt in Hastings.

THIS PAGE: A dormant volcanic crater, Mount Pouera was used as a fort in ancient times.

OPPOSITE (FROM TOP): During spring, blossoming trees transform the rural landscape into a burst of frothy pink and white colours; nephrite jade is highly valued by the Maoris, and it plays an important role in their culture.

a mighty land

New Zealand's main volcanic heartland runs through the centre of the North Island, stretching from Mount Ruapehu in the Tongariro National Park, through the Rotorua Lake District out to White Island in the Bay of Plenty, and the Taupo Volcanic Zone. However, volcanic activity is by no means confined to these areas. Auckland is built amongst 48 small volcanic cones, and boasts Rangitoto Island—the city's largest volcanic cone; its formation was witnessed by local Maori when the volcano erupted 600 years ago. Further south is Mount Taranaki (also known as Mount Egmont), with its near-perfect volcanic cone often being compared to that of the snow-capped Mount Fuji in Japan. There is also evidence of volcanic activity in the South Island, but it is comparatively marginal.

In the South Island, the Southern Alps are home to New Zealand's most precious materials—nephrite jade, or greenstone, also known by the Maori as pounamu. Rare and beautiful, greenstone is formed from the thick silvers of exotic rock which exist deep below the earth's crust. This stone holds great spiritual significance for the Maori people. Before the Europeans' arrival, it was the hardest material known to Maoris and was used for making tools, weapons and ornamentation.

bright, sunshiny days

New Zealand's climate ranges from temperate to subtropical—it is generally mild and equable with plenty of sunshine, ample rain and few extremes of heat and cold. However, because of the extensive mountain ranges, there is a great deal of regional variation. The weather from October onwards is warm, with summer technically starting in December. Some of the best weather conditions are in February and March, while early April is gloriously colourful. On both the North and South Islands, it gets wetter in the west than in the east; the mountains block the moisture-laden clouds blowing in from the Tasman Sea. It is usually a little cooler in the South Island than in the North, although in central Otago and on the east coast of the South Island, which are shielded by the Southern Alps, temperature variations can be likened to those of continental climates.

tales of the beginning

According to Maori mythology, New Zealand was 'fished up' by the demigod, Maui. One day Maui went out fishing with his five brothers. Using his magic fish hook, Maui caught a huge fish. This fish became the North Island, while the canoe in which he was sitting in became the South Island.

New Zealand's recent history is brief, though eventful. The last of the world's significant landmasses to be colonised, New Zealand is a land of immigrants. The origins of the country's first settlers are shrouded in mystery; one theory is that they were Polynesians who could have started their journey in Asia. By exploration and settlement in the islands of the South Pacific, these pioneers eventually—by planning or through sheer chance—came across New Zealand. The earliest estimates of human arrival in New Zealand are around 700 BCE, though solid archaeological evidence points to the period around 1200 CE. Maori legend has it that a mighty Polynesian voyager named Kupe discovered a great uninhabited land he called 'Aotearoa' (or 'land of the long white cloud') around 950 CE. Kupe is said to have then returned to his homeland, Hawaiki, where he told of his adventures. Four centuries later, a fleet of canoes, guided by Kupe's directions, set sail for the land he had discovered.

THIS PAGE: An aerial view of the Bay of Islands, in the Northland region of the North Island.
OPPOSITE (FROM TOP): In honour of Captain James Cook, a statue of him was erected in Gisborne; according to Maori legend, New Zealand had been discovered by Polynesians in a fleet of canoes.

european exploration

Explaining the two distinct Polynesian cultures has proved perplexing: in the first period of settlement (known as Moa Hunter or Archaic Maori), the way of living was relatively simple and appeared nomadic. In the second period (Classic Maori), there was a distinct stone-age culture. It was this society that greeted the arrival of the Europeans.

European voyagers began exploring the South Pacific region in the 16th century, taking 300 years to locate all of its islands. However, it is not known who actually first discovered Aotearoa, though it is recorded that in 1642, a Dutch explorer named Abel Tasman, landed at Golden Bay (originally named Murderers' Bay) on the north coast of the South Island. His visit was brief, and interaction with the local Maori ended in bloodshed and the loss of four crew members.

the lure of a new world

A hundred years later in 1769, Captain James Cook sighted the east coast of New Zealand. He was not alone; the French, led by Jean de Surville, also arrived around the same period. Both parties managed to establish communication with the locals, and after a succession of visits, permanent contact with the outside world was established. Over the next 10 years, Cook and his contemporaries opened up the Pacific entirely, and traders soon became based there.

making history

In 1840, New Zealand became an official British colony. The Treaty of Waitangi was drawn up between the British Government and the Maoris, and this is considered the founding document of New Zealand. The downside of this document is its inaccuracies. Maori was essentially a spoken rather than a written language, so despite the fact that there was a Maori version, it was not necessarily understood by the chiefs who signed it. In addition, when the English and Maori versions are compared, there are a number of discrepancies. These differences have led to controversy which still continues today.

Hopeful Europeans soon began to arrive thick and fast, and planned settlements were established. Despite the turmoil caused by the New Zealand Wars (also referred to as the Maori Wars or the Land Wars), which began in 1860 because of land conflicts, and continued throughout the decade, New Zealand's economy mostly managed to boom. The discovery of gold, together with the highly lucrative wool export prices, created a frenzy of economic activity.

an independent identity

For a long time, New Zealand was economically intertwined with Britain, being recognised as her 'bread-basket'. However, when the United Kingdom joined the European Union in 1973, these relations cooled slightly after Britain began to take supplies from other countries, leaving New Zealand with no choice but to find fresh markets for exporting its goods. Soon, social changes occurred and new foreign policies developed—policies that would come to define the New Zealand of today (for example, its anti-nuclear weapon stance). Gradually, New Zealand grew into far more than just an extension of Britain.

king and country

Ties with Britain remained strong, as exemplified by the show of solidarity during the First World War. Despite being a nation of only around 1 million, about 100,000 troops were sent to Europe to assist the British Empire. Close to 60,000 of them were killed. For such a small country, the losses suffered by New Zealand were devastating, particularly during the battle of Gallipoli, where large numbers of soldiers died. However, for the ANZAC (Australian and New Zealand Army Corps) troops involved, the Gallipoli campaign played an important part in fostering a sense of national identity. The tragedy of the Great War did not deter New Zealand from participating in the next World War, where once again, many troops were drafted in to assist the allies. Presently, the New Zealand Defence Force consists of three branches: the army, navy and air force.

leisurely pace of life

While it is impossible to generalise about a totally diverse group of people, it is widely thought that New Zealanders are some of the friendliest people a traveller could meet. This could perhaps be due to a more relaxed outlook: the pace of life in New Zealand is largely quite laid-back. New Zealanders tend to be proud of their country, convinced that they live in one of the most beautiful countries in the world.

growing up and away

New Zealand's parliament—based on the Statutes of Westminster—pays allegiance to the British sovereign through its Governor-General, the Queen's representative in New Zealand. There are aspects of the country that will strike a visitor as seeming British. For example, although both English and Maori are the official languages, the former is mostly spoken. However, despite many similarities, it is quite clear that this country is a world apart from Europe. New Zealand is an exotic land influenced by people of many different cultures assimilated into one, giving rise to a distinct New Zealand cultural identity.

THIS PAGE: The Parliament House of New Zealand is located in Wellington, and its southern wing is commonly known as 'The Beehive' because of its shape.

OPPOSITE (FROM TOP): A land of many cultures, Maori children are presenting a performance art item known as the kapa haka, which consists of Maori song and dances; toy figurines of soldiers re-enact the scene of troops marching to do battle.

While the Maori language is not widely spoken, it is often exclusively used on maraes.

a melting pot

The overwhelming majority of the inhabitants of New Zealand are of European descent (collectively known as Pakeha), with Maori people making up the second-largest group. There is also a significant population that has originated from the Pacific Islands, and a sizable Asian contingent.

Although the majority of the Europeans can trace their roots back to Britain, the passage of time has gradually diluted their links to what was once their homeland. Maori traditions are adhered to more by some than others, but there is a general respect and understanding for them, regardless of the ethnicity of the New Zealander. While the Maori language is not widely spoken, it is often exclusively used on maraes (Maori meeting houses and associated buildings). There are also certain Maori words that are commonly used in everyday conversation. Many landmarks in New Zealand have Maori names. The Polynesian population has largely settled in Auckland, giving the city a distinctly Pacific flavour, and a larger Polynesian population than in any other city in the South Pacific.

THIS PAGE (FROM TOP): Maori performers doing the haka, a traditional form of Maori dance that is often used during sporting activities and cultural performances; contemporary Maori art pieces which depict traditional motifs and shapes are highly popular among tourists.

OPPOSITE: An intricately-carved wooden structure in a replica village at the Maori Arts and Crafts Institute in Rotorua.

time-honoured traditions

It would be wrong to assume that the arts, crafts and traditions of modern day New Zealand have been derived purely from Maori roots, though their beliefs have certainly had a strong influence and impact. The Maori culture harks back to its Pacific Islands inheritance, with many of the ancient skills—wood, bone and stone carving, as well as plaiting and weaving—still thriving. The Maori language was not originally a written one: thus, oratory chants, songs and dances were, and still are, ways of passing on ancestral knowledge.

While the haka performed by the All Blacks is probably the most well-known ritual of challenge, there are equally celebrated forms of welcome and farewell. The poi dance is famously elegant—it is carried out with poi balls stuffed with reeds and covered with woven flax fibre, though its performance is restricted to women.

Another distinctive feature of the Maori culture is the moko (tattoo); traditional sites on the body are still used for such purposes. For men, it is the full facial area, while for women, their lips and chin. There has been a resurgence of Maori art recently, with many contemporary artists—both Maori and Pakeha—drawing on tradition for inspiration in music, fashion, sculpture and painting.

art of a nation

New Zealand has certainly produced its fair share of internationally acclaimed artists. Charles Frederick Goldie achieved fame with his portraits of the Maoris; Francis Hodgkins is another early 20th-century artist worthy of mention. More recently during the 1930–40s, Colin McCahon and Toss Woollaston have taken their places in New Zealand's art history. Among celebrated Maori artists are names such as Ralph Hotere, Para Matchett, Fred Graham and Shona Rapira Davies.

Some great New Zealand literary icons include well-known writers like Katherine Mansfield, Dame Ngaio Marsh, Janet Frame, Frank Sargeson and poet James K. Baxter. Witi Ihimaera and Keri Hulme (whose novel *The Bone People* won

THIS PAGE: Flock Hill, the location where the culminative battle scene of The Chronicles of Narnia was filmed. Flock Hill lies on private land, but tour groups can obtain permission to visit.

OPPOSITE (FROM TOP): Reflecting the quirky architectural styles in New Zealand, this house is built on what is described as 'the steepest residential street in the world' in Dunedin; Dame Kire Te Kanawa, an internationally famous New Zealand opera singer, in the making of her music video.

the International Booker Prize) have also achieved recent successes. Alan Duff's best-selling first novel in 1995, *Once Were Warriors* was made into a powerful film exposing the turbulence of sections of Maori society.

a rising star

However, it is through the medium of film that New Zealand has become widely appreciated on the international arts circuit. Movie directors like Jane Campion, Lee Tamahori and Peter Jackson have been hugely successful (via their films) in exposing New Zealand to be a country of inordinate beauty. Campion's *The Piano* was a platform, not just for the New Zealand countryside, but also a launch pad for young New Zealand actress Anna Paquin and the already-established Kiwi actor Sam Neill. Other films have followed, with New Zealand providing the theme for films such as *Whale Rider*, *River Queen*, *The World's Fastest Indian* and *Sione's Wedding*, and the backdrop for scenes in *Vertical Limit*, *The Last Samurai*, *The Chronicles of Narnia*, *King Kong*, and most famously, *The Lord of the Rings* trilogy.

rhyme + reason

Music has always been inextricably interwoven with the Maori culture, but on a commercial level New Zealand has picked up pace as of late. Dame Kiri Te Kanawa, New Zealand's world-famous opera singer, as well as local bands like Spilt Enz and Crowded House, are held in high esteem and enjoy wide success. Bic Runga, a singer-songwriter, whose achingly resonant vocals are proudly cherished, is one of the highest-selling New Zealand artists of recent times.

    There is a thriving contemporary Maori music, hip-hop and garage-rock scene, and some great venues in which to see performances. Musically, New Zealand's cross of cultures has been tapped, and has resulted in great things.

THIS PAGE: *The reflection of Auckland's Sky Tower on a commercial building.*

OPPOSITE (FROM TOP): *The Ngaruawahia Regatta, a series of boat races, is annually held at the Turangawaewae Marae on Waikato River; members from the All Blacks national team performing the 'haka', a pre-match ritual.*

mix + match

The architecture of New Zealand is an eclectic mix: ample space plays an important factor in the way houses are styled and developed. Another feature is the predominant use of timber as a primary building material. With earthquake risk a consideration, height and construction have generally been constrained, and single-level dwellings are common in urban and suburban areas. The mix of structures ranges from the intricately carved marae to gracious colonial dwellings; the weatherboard homes synonymous with mass housing to the newer houses that have drawn on the minimalist lines of modernism for inspiration.

The maraes found dotted across the countryside are loaded with symbolism. Single gable roofs are supported on posts that have been sunk into the ground; these posts have been elaborately carved and are a truly beautiful display of craftsmanship and tradition. The porch bargeboards denote the arms of the ancestors, the ridgepole the tribal backbone, and the rafters the ribs of family lineage.

By the 1900s, bay-fronted villas were the standard form of housing for the Europeans. Generally constructed from timber weatherboard with corrugated iron or clay tile roofs, some of these homes were plain and functional. The more elaborate designs were wonderfully picturesque, with many ornately decorated with pierced wood or cast iron fretwork decoration, stained glass windows and verandahs. Out in the countryside, the homesteads of wealthy farmers also drew upon the highly decorative touches of the Victorian era. Sprawling mansions were often grandiose and ostentatious in design and décor.

Housing styles were generally imported from elsewhere; inspiration was drawn from Britain's other colonies, California and the Mediterranean. These latter two styles are very much apparent in the infrastructure built from the 1930–40s. By the 1970s, innovative and quirky designs gained popularity. Today, various incongruous constructions can be found around the country. It is also standard procedure for Kiwis to build their own homes; subdivisions of land are developed, and sections purchased. Within these, an individual can construct the home of his own choice.

game for anything

It is not an exaggeration to say that a typical New Zealander's life will incorporate some form of activity. New Zealand is a nation that is immensely proud of its competitive sporting achievements. Sports have always been an important part of New Zealand life. Early Maori arrivals partook in wrestling, running, canoeing and surfing competitions. European settlers, who arrived later, discovered a host of different sporting activities available to them, with the climate and terrain lending itself to outdoor pursuits.

This has led to New Zealand earning an international reputation for sporting prowess. When the population of the country is taken into consideration, the years of achievement on a world level and the number of high-ranking sportspeople who have come from New Zealand are truly remarkable.

rugby mania

Top on the list of sporting passions in New Zealand is rugby. It is not uncommon for children to start playing from as young as four years old. This is most definitely a game to be watched, played and supported by the entire family.

The New Zealand Rugby Union is predominant, and the members of the All Blacks national team are revered as heroes. There are no class or race barriers in this game, and it transcends all cultural and socio-economic divides: Pakeha, Maori and Polynesian Islander representatives can be seen on the teams.

The All Blacks trademark black uniform with a silver fern emblazoned on the chest was already in place by 1888, when the native team from New Zealand toured Britain. Rugby mania is by no means restricted to All Blacks games. Other big events include the Super 14 tournament, with teams from Australia and South Africa; the Bledisloe Cup—an ongoing fight to the finish between Australia and New Zealand; the Tri-Nations with Australia, New Zealand and Great Britain; and the National Provincial Championship.

sports for all seasons

Apart from rugby, there is still plenty of time to set aside to watch and take part in other activities. Netball is a leading winter sport for women; and men, women and children unerringly support its national team (the Silver Ferns). Cricket is the summer's team sport of choice, with the Black Caps representing the country internationally.

The mountainous terrain of New Zealand makes it ideal for winter activities such as skiing and snowboarding. Some of the best winter sports can be enjoyed on the slopes of Mount Ruapehu in the North Island, and Queenstown and Wanaka in the South. For the more adventurous, extreme sports such as heli-skiing and glacier skiing have been added to the repertoire. Rock climbing, mountaineering and caving are also popular and well-organised sports. New Zealand is fast becoming known for its mountain biking opportunities, with enthusiasts claiming it offers some of the best trails in the world.

There is no doubt that New Zealand affords both its natives and tourists an inordinate choice of water sports—diving, rafting, kayaking, water-skiing and wakeboarding facilities are all easily accessible. With some of the best fishing in the world on offer, anglers travel from far and wide to cast their lines in the waters. The lakes and rivers of the central North Island provide rich pickings for trout anglers, with world-record big game fish having been landed predominantly in the Bay of Islands. Sailing is widely enjoyed, as most New Zealanders live within easy access of the water. On a competitive level, the America's Cup is a challenge that leaves the nation holding its breath in the hopes that the Cup will be restored to them once more.

THIS PAGE: Team New Zealand taking part in the America's Cup, one of the most famous and prestigious regatta in the sport of sailing.

OPPOSITE (FROM LEFT): Skiing, a popular winter sport, is especially challenging in the Remarkables skifield near Queenstown, which is noted for its steep terrains and long off-piste runs; a pair of snowmen 'guard' a half-buried set of snow skis and a snowboard.

adrenalin activities

New Zealand is undoubtedly the home of extreme sports as well, with adventure tourism taking off with the launch of the Kawarau Bridge Bungee site by A.J. Hackett in Queenstown in 1988. Queenstown is still a hub of heart-stopping activities, but there are plenty of adrenalin-pumping sports on offer elsewhere—an array of exciting options guaranteed to get the blood rushing. From traditional sports like canoeing, mountain biking and skiing to the more adventurous ones like snowboarding, paragliding, kitesurfing or skydiving, the common thread that binds these activities together is the spectacular surroundings in which they take place. New Zealand, with its diversity of scenery and varying terrain, is being recognised as a world-class venue for many of these sports.

life in the fast lane

The thrill of bungee jumping is the sensation of hurtling towards the ground at a vast speed. Jumps can take place from platforms of varying heights—the more scenic the spot, the better. Among the most well-known places to indulge in this activity are the Kawarau Bridge and Skippers Canyon in Queenstown, Taupo, and the Auckland Harbour Bridge. Jumpers are each attached to a huge rubber cord that has been strapped around their ankles, ensuring that safety has been meticulously taken care of.

Auckland offers thrill seekers the Sky Jump, which involves leaping from the Sky Tower, covering a distance of 192 m (630 ft) in 16 seconds. Unlike a bungee jump (where the jumper plunges down head-first), jumpers gain their adrenalin rush from plummeting 75 km/h (46 miles/h) for most of the distance, before slowing down to land gently on the ground. Safety precautions are taken care of: the 'flying suit', a full body harness and a jump cable are enough to reassure jumpers before they take the plunge.

Based in Rotorua, Zorbing is a relatively new recreational activity, though it is probably more peculiar rather than terrifying. Travellers game for a new experience are squeezed through a small hole into a huge transparent plastic ball. Buckets of water are sloshed inside the ball for good measure, before it is given a hearty shove off a hill.

THIS PAGE: The Ledge Bungee in Queenstown is equipped with a 'runway'.

OPPOSITE (FROM LEFT): Abseiling 100 m (328 ft) into the Waitomo Caves before walking, swimming or climbing back up past stalactites and stalagmites is an experience not to be missed; Zorbing is a quirky sporting activity that entails one to roll downhill inside a white, double-hulled sphere called a Zorbus.

water world

The white water rafting opportunities in New Zealand are superb; the Kaituna River just outside Rotorua claims to be the highest commercially rafted waterfall in the world. The drop over the Tutea Falls is 7 m (23 ft), but there are plenty of other adrenalin-inducing moments along the way as the raft zips its way through the narrow gorge.

Cave rafting, or black water rafting as it is called in Waitomo, involves slipping into a wetsuit, donning a hard hat and floating through a dark underground world in a rubber inner tube. Unexpected drops and rocky chutes all add to the excitement of this journey. The same activity is available at Westport and Greymouth.

climb every mountain

Known as the arena of the great outdoors, New Zealand is every keen tramper's paradise. There are countless tracks to hike, to suit varying levels of expertise. The glory of trekking in New Zealand is the diversity of the scenery; it is possible to experience coastal ambles and exhilarating climbs up snow-capped volcanic peaks, all within a relatively close geographical area. Whether it is an hour-long tramp or a week in the bush, it is guaranteed to thrill even the most dedicated of walking enthusiasts.

New Zealand is well equipped to deal with hikers who flock to enjoy its exquisite countryside. In addition to its well-marked tracks, a network of huts can be found along many of the walks, although these vary in degrees of comfort. The Department of Conservation (DOC) maintains these huts and campsites. It also runs both local offices and a highly comprehensive website, where details of the various tramps are readily available online.

the greatest walks of all

The most popular organised tramping routes are called the 'Great Walks'. Numbering nine in total (although one is technically a river trip), each individual route is exceptionally beautiful: hence, their unerring popularity.

Perhaps the most famous Great Walk is the Milford Track in the South Island. A four-day, 54-km (34-mile) tramp through the enchanting Fiordland National Park will take travellers along a journey of alpine scenery, river valleys, glaciers and waterfalls. The terrain can be rough, and at times challenging, but venturing forth into this untouched wilderness is definitely an experience not to be missed.

In the same region lies the Kepler Track. Taking four to five days to complete, this 67 km (42 miles) excursion is less popular than the Milford route, but by no means any less sensational. The walk involves a mountain climb that affords breathtaking views of alpine, lake and river scenery. The Routeburn Track also traverses the Fiordland National Park. However, the route is only 40 km (25 miles) long, and takes only three days to finish.

Another Great Walk in the South Island is the three-day Rakiura Track on Stewart Island. Taking trampers along the coast and through forest, this Great Walk is a bird lover's paradise. At the top end of the South Island is the Abel Tasman Coastal Track. This track is hugely popular with trampers as the easy three- to five-day walk can be split into even smaller segments. Not far off in the Kahurangi National Park is the more demanding Heaphy Track—the five days worth of hiking through forest are tough but exhilarating.

THIS PAGE: The Tongariro Crossing, a walking trail in the Tongariro National Park, consists of a fascinating hike past colourful crater lakes, lava formations and volcanic steam vents.

OPPOSITE: A magical world of moss-covered trees and pure mountain water, the Routeburn Track provides a surreal experience for trekkers attempting this Great Walk.

The North Island is home to the famous Tongariro Northern Circuit. This tramp through the volcanic landscape of Tongariro traverses spectacular terrain, affording one with views of snowy peaks, glacial lakes, craters and hot springs. For trampers who are unable to spare the four days needed to complete the Circuit, they can opt for the one-day Tongariro Crossing, known as the most spectacular day walk in New Zealand. Both hikes are prone to adverse weather, so walkers are advised to check the conditions first. The Lake Waikaremoana Track in Te Urewa National Park offers trampers great views of the lake and surrounding bush, and takes a relatively relaxing three or four days to complete. The Whanganui Journey is counted as a Great Walk, but is in fact a canoe trip. Meandering down the Whanganui River through the National Park, it is a phenomenal way to experience the countryside.

something for everyone

In addition to the famous routes, there are countless other trails waiting to be discovered. The Cape Brett Track in Northland is a less known, but wonderfully scenic route. Other Northland favourites are Cape Reinga and the Ninety Mile Beach. There are also some fabulous routes in the Coromandel area, while the challenging terrain of the Tararua Ranges outside Wellington city attracts the most dedicated enthusiasts. The South Island is loved by hikers, with the Aoraki/Mount Cook area offering countless options. The more adventurous can head for the Copland Track, which makes its way towards Fox Glacier: crossing a glacier at high altitude is just one of the thrills, and mountaineering equipment and experience are imperative. The Matukituki Valley in Mount Aspiring National Park offers a number of fabulous walks; the Kaikoura Coast Track has rugged coastal scenery and is an easy three-day walk. There are also a multitude of tracks in the Fiordland area, which is one of the most beloved walking areas in the country.

THIS PAGE: *A multitude of mountain streams provide quick relief for hikers who opt to try out the Copland Track, which snakes through the rainforests on the South Island's west coast to Mount Cook.*

OPPOSITE (CLOCKWISE FROM TOP): *Washed ashore are two Sunflower Starfish from a tide pool near Hokitika; footsteps left behind on a beach; the kiwi is a species of small flightless birds endemic to New Zealand, of which all are endangered due to their size and inability to fly.*

flora + fauna: a slice of heaven

New Zealand is surrounded on all sides by great expanses of ocean; its regions vary widely in environment and climate. As a result, this unique environment has led to the lack of serious predators, thus having a due impact on wildlife. Evolving to suit their surroundings, some species of birds lost their ability to fly, and being amply fed, they gained unusual size as a result.

About 80 per cent of the flora, nearly all of the insects and around a quarter of the birds are found nowhere else in the world. Most notable about the New Zealand fauna is that there are no native land mammals apart from a few species of bats. Furthermore, there are no snakes and only two types of poisonous spiders.

feathery friends

New Zealand is most well-known for the kiwi, a small flightless bird. A comical creature, it is roughly the size of a chicken and lives in dense bush and forest. The kiwi is nocturnal and shy, and it is equipped with a long bill that has nostrils at the end—perfectly designed to sniff out worms and underground insects. There are currently five accepted species of kiwis in New Zealand: the Roroa, Little Spotted Kiwi, Rowi, Tokoeka and North Island Brown Kiwi.

The kiwi has become something of a national emblem. A fruit is named after it, and so are brands and sports teams. It is also the global nickname for the people of New Zealand. However, there are other less famous and less fortunate flightless birds. The kakapo (or native parrot) is now seriously endangered and has been moved to areas with no known predators. It has also been entered into a breeding programme in order to protect it. Another example is the moa. New Zealand was once home to a dozen species of this large bird, which ranged in height from 1 metre (3.3 ft) tall to twice the height of an ostrich. The first settlers hunted the moa mercilessly, and ultimately they became extinct.

the bountiful ocean

Ocean life is abundant, and the fish-rich waters are also home to an assortment of marine mammals. Various species of whales (like the enormous Sperm Whale), dolphins and seals are regularly spotted around the coastline. The New Zealand waters are home to the world's smallest—and possibly rarest—dolphin, the Hector Dolphin. These frisky creatures are endemic to the coastal regions, and are often found in groups of two to eigth.

footprints in the sand

The Polynesians made the first significant changes to the ecology. They burnt off huge areas of the forests and hunted wildlife. They also introduced the first two destructive mammals: the Polynesian rat and the dog. The Europeans, for their part, introduced a host of new phenomena imported from the northern hemisphere: birds, deciduous trees,

more rodents, cattle, sheep, pigs, deer, possums, goats and rabbits. These new introductions had a huge detrimental impact on both the fauna and flora of New Zealand; the damage to the land was considerable.

However, New Zealand remains an ecological paradise. It continues to boast some of the most impressive forest areas in the world (for example, the kauri forests of Northland, the broadleaf-podocarp forests in the central North Island and the ancient beech forests in the South Island). During the summer months, travellers will be able to see the beautiful scarlet flowers of the pohutukawa (known as the New Zealand Christmas Tree), and the Silver Fern, which is also another national symbol. Nearly half of the native plant species are alpine plants, many of which are only found in New Zealand. With its unique vegetation, unusual birdlife and wealth of marine life, this country remains in a league of its own.

OPPOSITE: Sealife is prolific in the oceans of New Zealand, where the bountiful amounts of underwater life are evident.

BELOW: A panoramic high-angle view of New Zealand's ecological landscape, seen from a pier on the Pounawea River.

the economy: a country practice

Despite its reputation as a great farming country, 85 per cent of the New Zealand population is actually urban. Nevertheless, agriculture is undoubtedly New Zealand's major industry—with meat, dairy and wool exports forming a large part of the market. Other important exports include timber products, fruit and fish. Over the years agricultural farming has been forced to diversify; while traditionally, pastoral farming has centred on sheep and cattle, other kinds of livestock such as deer, goats, pigs and poultry are becoming mainstays in the farming industry.

rich pickings

The mild sunny climate and fertile soils of the various coastal areas have given rise to a successful horticultural industry. Next to New Zealand lamb, kiwifruit is probably the most well-known export from this country. Grown primarily in the Bay of Plenty, New Zealand is at the forefront of the kiwifruit market. New Zealand apples are also widely distributed internationally, and although other pip fruits are exported, they are in far less significant quantities.

an experience to remember

Tourism has become a huge growth industry in New Zealand, and government officials are quick to acknowledge this fact. New Zealand offers travellers a totally unique package of unspoilt countryside and the chance to enjoy its remarkably relaxed way of living. The tourist boom has coincided with significant developments within New Zealand. New Zealand wines have increasingly become world-acclaimed, and a number of internationally-recognised chefs have both led and inspired a new wave of modern restaurants and eateries.

The discovery of New Zealand by the film industry has only served to further showcase its innate beauty. All of these factors have encouraged the development of more world-class accommodation, sleekly-operated activities and an improved infrastructure.

THIS PAGE (FROM TOP): Green apples floating in a washing tank after being plucked from the orchards; Te Puke, a horticultural town in the Bay of Plenty, is one of the two main areas in New Zealand which grows kiwifruit.

OPPOSITE: An evening view of Christchurch. The distinctive features of the Christchurch Cathedral can be seen.

...85 per cent of the New Zealand population is actually urban.

northisland

Three Kings Islands

Cape Reinga
North Cape
Te Kao
Great Exhibition Bay
Ninety Mile Beach
Houhora Heads
Karikari Peninsula
Cavalli Islands
Kaitaia
Bay of Islands
Kerikeri
Cape Brett
Paihia
Kaikohe
Russell
Opononi
Poor Knights Island
Hokianga Harbour
▲ 770
> Waipoua Lodge
> Paihia Beach Resort + Spa
Whangarei
Dargaville
Goat Island Marine Reserve
Little Barrier Island
Kaiwaka
Great Barrier Island
Wellsford
Kaipara Harbour
Kawau Island
> The Castle Matakana
Rangitoto Island
Cuvier Island
Helensville
Cape Colville
Mercury Islands
Takapuna
Hauraki Gulf
Waiheke Island
Auckland
> SKYCITY Grand Hotel
> The Villa Book
> Heritage Hotel + Spa du Vin
Manukau
Coromandel Peninsula
Slipper Island
> Delamore Lodge
> The Boatshed
> The Villa Book
Thames

Paeroa
Waihi
Mayor Island
Huntly
Matakana Island
Cape Runaway
Ngaruawahia
Motiti Island
White Island
East Cape
Raglan
Hamilton
Tauranga
Hicks Bay
> Accolades Boutique Hotel
Cambridge
Bay of Plenty
> Nicara Lakeside Lodge
Kawhia
Wakatane
> Peppers on the Point
Opotiki
▲ 1754
Ruatoria
> Treetops Lodge + Wilderness Estate
> The Villa Book
Waitomo Caves
Te Kuiti
Rotorua
Tokomaru Bay
> Lodge at 199
> Solitaire Lodge
> Clearwater Cruises
Tolaga Bay
> The Villa Book
> Huka Lodge
Taupo
Gisborne
North Taranaki Bight
Lake Taupo
Poverty Bay
Taumarunui
Lake Waikaremoana
Turangi
Tarawera
New Plymouth
▲ 1978 Mt. Tongariro
Wairoa
Mahia Peninsula
2518
Tongariro National Park
▲ 2291 Mt. Ngauruhoe
Egmont Cape
▲ Mt. Taranaki
▲ 2797 Mt. Ruapehu
Hawke Bay
Opunake
Cape Kidnappers
Portland Island
Stratford
Ohakune
Napier
Hawera
Whanganui National Park
Taihape
Hastings
South Taranaki Bight
▲ 1733
Wanganui
Waipawa
Waipukurau
Feilding
Dannevirke
Woodville
Palmerston North
Cape Turnagain
> HELiPRO
Levin
> Peppers Martinborough Hotel
Kapiti Island
Paraparaumu
▲ 1571
Masterton
Upper Hutt
Lower Hutt
Wellington

T a s m a n S e a

South Island

Cook Strait

Cape Palliser

S o u t h P a c i f i c O c e a n

N

Legend

≡ Highway
▬ Main Road
⊕ Airport
   Water
● 3000–4000 m
● 2000–3000 m
● 1000–2000 m
● 500–1000 m
● 200–500 m

0 km   60   120   180 km

north island

The North Island is home to Wellington, the capital city of New Zealand, and Auckland, the largest city in the country. Two-thirds of the 4 million or so New Zealanders live on the North Island, which is also the centre of Maori and Polynesian culture.

Known for its subtropical temperatures and varied scenery, the North's most dramatic features are the Volcanic Plateau and the geothermal activity that characterise this central area. Although Rotorua is the heartland of this activity, bubbling springs can also be found elsewhere in the region. Despite the North Island's rocky centre, the lands surrounding it are lush, green and fertile, giving rise to prime agricultural and horticultural areas, and fresh produce. Framing the rolling hills and vales are beautiful beaches; indeed, some of the best coastlines in the country can be found on the North Island. At the very tip of the island, there are sand dunes and stretches of isolated beach that are nothing short of breathtaking.

auckland region

Auckland is both a city and a region. The area encompasses some fabulous scenery which includes outer islands, beaches and vineyards. The beaches of the west coast are regarded by Aucklanders as 'the real' New Zealand. Rugged landscapes and untouched coves typify the area, and among the favourite coastal spots are Piha, Bethells and Muriwai Beaches. With its sweeping harbour and island-dotted coastline, it is little surprise that Auckland is often referred to as the 'City of Sails'. However, it is not just yachting enthusiasts who are drawn to this region. Boasting fabulous restaurants, boutique stores and quaint colonial residential suburbs, Auckland is an alluring city that is easy to fall in love with.

The Viaduct Harbour area in Auckland is all about aesthetics. Smart apartments, sleek hotels, sophisticated restaurants and buzzing bars accessorise this waterfront spot, and the result is a glorious hang-out zone for locals and tourists alike. At night the area comes alive, and on a balmy summer evening this is the perfect place to relax and

PAGE 38: New Zealand is as rich in colour below water as above it. A cluster of starfish highlights its mesmerising ocean life.

THIS PAGE: The famous Sky Tower dominates the Auckland cityscape; it is particularly striking by night when it is lit up.

OPPOSITE: The Motuarohia Island in Northland is distinguished by its two glorious lagoons. Situated in the Bay of Islands, it is the first island to be seen once out on the waters from Paihia or Russell.

enjoy the city vibe. In central Auckland, many other exciting tourist attractions can be found. The Auckland War Memorial Museum at the Domain houses a fascinating collection of exhibits. A visit to the cloud-piercing Sky Tower is considered a must. Rising to an impressive height of 328 m (1,076 ft), it is reputed to be the tallest tower in the Southern Hemisphere. Its 360-degree views of the cityscape are spectacular, and gazing down through the glass panel floor is enough to make the sturdiest stomach somersault.

shopping paradise

Queen Street is where the bulk of the standard retailers can be found. Nearby, Chancery is a chic paved walkway crammed with select designer outlets. Shoppers often travel outside the central business district to Newmarket, where Karen Walker, one of New Zealand's leading fashion designer label can be found, or further away from the city centre to malls such as Sylvia Park or Botany Downs. Karen Walker is a New Zealand-born fashion designer known for her original and unpretentious style, and her clothing labels are carried worldwide, including major cities like New York, London and Hong Kong.

The suburban area of Ponsonby is filled with the kitsch and the quirky. Once the more risqué side of the city, Ponsonby has since developed into an artsy stronghold. Its streets are lined with shops offering everything from furnishings to fashion, alongside cafés, bars and restaurants. Aside from Ponsonby, there are other areas around Auckland which are a pleasure to explore. For example, the suburbs of Grey Lynn and Herne Bay are lined with glorious colonial villas.

peaks + views

Also within close proximity is Mount Eden where the famed One Tree Hill, formerly the site of a large Maori fortification, can be found. A reminder of Auckland's volcanic terrain, the views from One Tree Hill are worth making the trip for. The region is dotted with as many as 48 volcanic cones. The most recent and largest eruption took place around 600 years ago at Rangitoto Island, which is visible from the city.

Auckland's coastal highlights are numerous. Just over the Harbour Bridge is the North Shore, where many of its pretty bays and beaches can be found. Devonport, a seaside suburb of Auckland, is a 10-minute ferry ride from Auckland's Ferry Building, and offers a rich and diverse history. It is well-known for its relaxed village ambience and boutique-styled beaches.

THIS PAGE (FROM TOP): *A model parading the latest fashion wear from a Karen Walker collection; the luxurious suites of The Boatshed hotel have panoramic views of the Hauraki Gulf.*

OPPOSITE: *Karen Walker, one of the country's foremost fashion designers, has stores in the up-market Auckland areas of Newmarket and O'Connell Street, as well as Wellington.*

so near, yet so far

The islands of the Hauraki Gulf are gathered between the Coromandel Peninsula in the east and Auckland to the west in a stretch of water that's a favourite with boating enthusiasts. They are also magnets for day-trippers and nature lovers; many Aucklanders use these islands as a welcome respite from the hustle and bustle of city life.

Waiheke Island is the most acclaimed of the islands. It is also the second-largest. Only a 35-minute ferry ride across from the city, it is easily commutable for city workers. In addition, a growth spurt of restaurants and luxury accommodation there attracts a steady stream of visitors. The island is also home to lush landscapes, sweeping beaches, secluded anchorages, rocky headlands and rolling hills dotted with established vineyards; prestigiously designed houses look down on picturesque bays. The streets of Waiheke's main settlement of Oneroa are lined with chic cafés; visits to this village are as much a treat for the taste buds as they are for the aesthetics.

rustic charm

Great Barrier Island is the largest of the islands in the Hauraki Gulf, stretching 40 km (25 miles) from its north to south. Rough and rugged, it is part of an island chain marking the outer edge of the arena. A small population lives on the island today, treasuring its peace and tranquillity. On the island there are tracks to tramp, isolated beaches to enjoy, plus fabulous surfing, mountain biking and diving opportunities. A range of accommodation on the island means that the destination can be enjoyed by a cross-section of travellers. A regular ferry-service runs from Auckland; the journey takes around two hours. Flights are also available. Nearby, Little Barrier Island is mountainous and densely forested. Known to be one of the more isolated islands in the Gulf, it is not inhabited, though the Maori used to live there in earlier times. This island is a flora and fauna reserve where an abundance of rare native birds and tuatara (prehistoric lizard-like creatures) are known to roam freely. Visitors need to obtain a permit before landing.

THIS PAGE: For Kiwis, the love of adrenalin-pumping activities starts at an early age. Jumping from rocks and bridges is preparation for the more adult thrill-seeking experiences.

OPPOSITE: Snorkelling and fishing opportunities abound in this area.

step back in time

Other much-visited islands in the Gulf Harbour are the Rangitoto and Kawau Islands, both of which are in the inner area and are served by a regular ferry or by charter boats. The summit walk on Rangitoto Island affords superb views of Auckland, the northern bays and of the Gulf itself. Kawau Island is most famous for being home to the Mansion House, the country home of early governors. This elegant residence is open to the general public, and a reminder of colonial New Zealand.

Just north of Auckland is Goat Island. It was here that the very first marine reserve was established. As a result, the surrounding waters are full of ocean life: snappers, blue maomaos and red moki are but a few of the species of fish to be seen. Snorkelling and diving will uncover even more exotic finds.

northland region

Often known as the 'Far North' or 'The Winterless North' because of its temperate climate, the Northland occupies a large stretch of the 285 km- (177 mile-) long North Auckland Peninsula. It is bounded on its sides by the Tasman Sea and the Pacific Ocean. Here is where some of New Zealand's best beaches can be found, with vast stretches of golden sands characterising its east coast, and sand dunes and breakers to the west. Along the west coast are two large inlets, the Kaipara and Hokianga Harbours.

Northland's landscape is predominantly rural, with farming and forestry industries occupying most of the land area. Although many of the region's kauri forests were felled during the 19th century, one such forest, the Waipoua Kauri Forest, still exists today. Located south of the Hokianga Harbour, this forest is home to New Zealand's largest kauri tree.

This region is also known to be a fishing enthusiast's paradise. Trips out at sea result in rich hauls of everything from snapper to kingfish, gurnard to John Dory. Leisurely strolls along the seashore at low tide often reveal fat, juicy mussels. Deep-sea divers will delight in plucking scallops and crayfish off the ocean bed.

...the Bay of Islands district in the heart of Northland is an area of enchanting beauty.

islands in the sun

A three-hour drive from Auckland, the Bay of Islands district in the heart of
Northland is an area of enchanting beauty. Located close to the northern tip
of the island, the warm, turquoise waters off its coastline are renowned
worldwide for offering great deep-sea fishing opportunities. It is also a
sanctuary for frolicking dolphins, and on occasion, pods of passing whales.

Whereas fishing was once the mainstay of this area, the tourist industry
now thrives. To complement the existing beach houses, B&Bs, motels and
hotels, luxury accommodations such as lodges, estates and even private
islands have been developed to offer visitors a unique and special
experience in this heavenly hideaway.

In the town of Paihia, the buzz of tourism hums most of the year round. When
one looks out across to the ocean, the views are breathtaking—tiny isles are
scattered across the water like confetti, and boats glide by in elegant formations.
Paihia is the perfect base for exploring the Bay of Islands, and an ideal place to
book an excursion—whether it be a fishing trip, a jet-boat ride out to the famous
Hole in the Rock, or swimming with dolphins.

from the beginning

Sometimes referred to as 'the birthplace of the nation', Northland is an area steeped
in history. Just a couple of kilometres north of Paihia is the spot where, on 6 February
1840, 46 Maori chiefs and representatives from Queen Victoria's government signed
the Treaty of Waitangi. This became the founding document for modern New
Zealand. The Treaty House and Waitangi Treaty Grounds are testament to the
importance of this momentous occasion.

Another historical stronghold in the area is the small colonial town of Russell.
Accessible via ferry from either Opua (vehicle passage) or Paihia (foot ferry), Russell is
inordinately picturesque. Under European settlement during the 19th century, the area

*THIS PAGE: The Waitangi House
bears huge historical
significance. The Treaty of
Waitangi signed here is the
controversial cornerstone of
Maori and Pakeha (European)
relations in New Zealand.*

*OPPOSITE: An aerial view of the
Bay of Islands, it is possible to
travel across to the picturesque
town of Russell by car or ferry
from the town of Opua.*

flourished. Known until 1844 as Kororareka, the Europeans made it their capital (before moving to Auckland and ultimately Wellington). While in the early days the region had thrived, the popularity of the area dwindled as the economy shifted further south. The legacy of colonial times is very much apparent—along the waterfront at Russell sits the Duke of Marlborough Hotel, which is believed to be the oldest pub in New Zealand.

places of interest

A little further up the east coast are the Cavalli Islands—one large and four smaller islands make up the main body of the group, with a number of additional isles peppering the ocean around them.

White sand beaches and turquoise waters are just part of the appeal of this area. Motukawanui is the largest island in the group; until recently the land was farmed. Now the island lies uninhabited, although it is possible to stay overnight on it. Diving opportunities in the vicinity are regarded to be among the best in New Zealand; the underwater scenery is made more appealing by the presence of the Greenpeace flagship, Rainbow Warrior, a dive wreck.

THIS PAGE: The Cavalli Beach House Retreat allows guests to enjoy great views from every room.

OPPOSITE (FROM LEFT): The Poor Knights Islands offer breathtaking underwater viewings of sponge gardens and gorgonian fields; biking along Ninety Mile Beach, which stretches from Aphipara to the tip of the North Island, is one way to see this spectacular area.

Further north, Doubtless Bay is an idyllic stretch of coastline; within this area are four small townships—one of which is Mangonui, a pretty little holiday spot.

Crossing over to the west coast, Cape Reinga is at the tip of the North Island, at the point where the Tasman Sea and Pacific Ocean meet. Between here and Kaitaia is a magnificent stretch of coast known as the Ninety Mile Beach. Belting along the sand in a four-wheel drive, or surfing on sand dunes on a bodyboard are exhilarating experiences. This area is soaked in

history and legend. Being one of the main locations of early Maori settlement, Hokianga Harbour is a place of significance to the northern tribes of Maori people. A little inland are the giant kauri trees of the ancient and mystical Waipoua Kauri Forest. Home to Tane Mahuta, the 'God of the Forest', New Zealand's tallest Kauri tree, is a symbol of past and present.

Back over on the east coast are the Poor Knights Islands. An established marine reserve, the islands' waters are wonderfully clear. This, together with the abundance of ocean life within, has earned this area the reputation of being one of the top 10 dive spots in the world. The islands themselves float in warm subtropical waters, and are carefully protected from human visitors in order to preserve the rare flora and fauna that grow and breed there.

waikato region

Waikato is best known for its lush green countryside and dairy farm industry. The city of Hamilton is the region's hub and it prides itself on its increasingly cosmopolitan reputation. The surf beaches of Raglan on its west coast attract countless visitors to this small seaside resort. Along the coastal route in this vicinity are beautiful landscapes to be savoured; there are excellent swimming and surfing opportunities as well.

One particularly quaint spot in the area is the small town of Cambridge—located just outside of Hamilton, and home to New Zealand's thoroughbred horse industry. However, one of the biggest attractions of Waikato are the Waitomo Caves. Displaying impressive glow-worm grottoes and limestone formations, the caves are also home to black water rafting. This activity mimics white water rafting, except that the adventure takes place underground and in the dark.

coromandel region

A destination that captures the essence of New Zealand, it is little wonder that the Coromandel Peninsula is a very popular destination for both locals and tourists alike. This beautiful, rugged area is best loved for its long stretches of soft snow-white sand. Expanses of lush bush land and the glorious bright-red-flowering pohutukawa trees further add to the stunning scenery.

beaches galore

A number of beaches dot the coastline, each with unique appeal and character. Hot Water Beach is so named because of the geothermal heated water that bubbles away under certain parts of the sand. Cooks Beach, with its perfect waters, is another spot that draws visitors in droves during the summer. New Chums Beach, north east of the Coromandel township, is a little off the beaten track and involves a walk to reach it, but its golden sands are the reward.

The town of Whangamata is the second-largest town on the peninsula. Its beach is hugely popular, particularly with families, for its crystal-clear waters, white sands and surfing facilities. The town is dotted with cafés and surf shops, and its wonderfully languid ambience will persuade visitors to stay longer.

natural attractions

Many of the towns in the Coromandel region are of historical interest, with heritage trails, local museums, Victorian architecture, and in some cases, remnants from the gold-mining and kauri-logging days. The gold-mining history of the area has been preserved in the scenic Karangahake Gorge, and the towns of Waihi, Thames and Coromandel. The Gorge is an impressive sight—its steep rock edges are breathtaking. A number of walking tracks will take trampers through beautiful native bush land.

A little further along the highway is Paeroa, a town that holds its place in Kiwi hearts as the supplier of the mineral waters used to make Lemon & Paeroa, an indigenous soft drink. This sweet fizzy pop has a taste that is impossible to put into words, and has to be sampled for its sheer novelty value.

While the gold-mining and timber days of the Coromandel Township are long gone, it is now establishing itself as one of New Zealand's main arts and crafts centres. Artists have been attracted to the area by the relaxed lifestyle and native bush setting, and some open their studios to visitors.

THIS PAGE (FROM TOP): The beaches along the Coromandel coastline are popular places for family outings or evening strolls; a huge replica bottle of Lemon & Paeroa reflects the popularity of this iconic soft drink.
OPPOSITE: While abseilling down into a massive shaft, one can admire the spectacular scenery of the Waitomo Caves.

bay of plenty region

The Bay of Plenty region incorporates a range of diverse landscapes, which include the white coastal sands of Mount Maunganui and the steaming thermal terrain of Rotorua. Tauranga, in the Western Bay of Plenty, is a harbourside city that attracts visitors to its wealth of activities. It is a thriving shopping and restaurant area, and there are opportunities for boating, surfing and deep-sea fishing.

Nearby, the seaside town of Mount Maunganui, with its stretch of wide beach and tempting surf, is hard to resist. The idyllic climate in the Bay of Plenty makes it perfect for fruit growing, and the gardens there brim with avocado and lemon trees. This is also the region famous for its kiwifruit; the town of Te Puke is often referred to as the 'Kiwifruit capital of the world'.

islands aplenty

There are a number of tiny islands scattered off the coastline of the Bay of Plenty. Some are privately owned; others are rocky wildlife sanctuaries. Several are well-visited tourist attractions. Mayor Island (or Tuhua) is a dormant volcano that lies around 35 km (22 miles) off the coast of Tauranga. Thick foliage covers its black obsidian summit; obsidian is a natural glass formed by the rapid cooling of silica rich lava. The two lakes—one green, the other black—that lie within a crater on the island are the island's main visual features. There are walking tracks through the crater valley and around the island. However, the northern coastline is a Department of Conservation (DOC) protected marine reserve. Charter boats run from Tauranga, and there is basic accommodation on the island.

Matakana Island is home to a small community, and is a short ferry ride from Tauranga. Floating in the aqua ocean, it presents a striking sight: thick, lush pine forest rimmed by perfect slivers of sandy beach. While these beaches are especially

THIS PAGE: A funfair in full swing at Mount Maunganui.
OPPOSITE: A shoal of jack mackerel fish cluster in the depths of the ocean.

...there are opportunities for boating, surfing and deep-sea fishing.

...the spiritual home of the Maori...

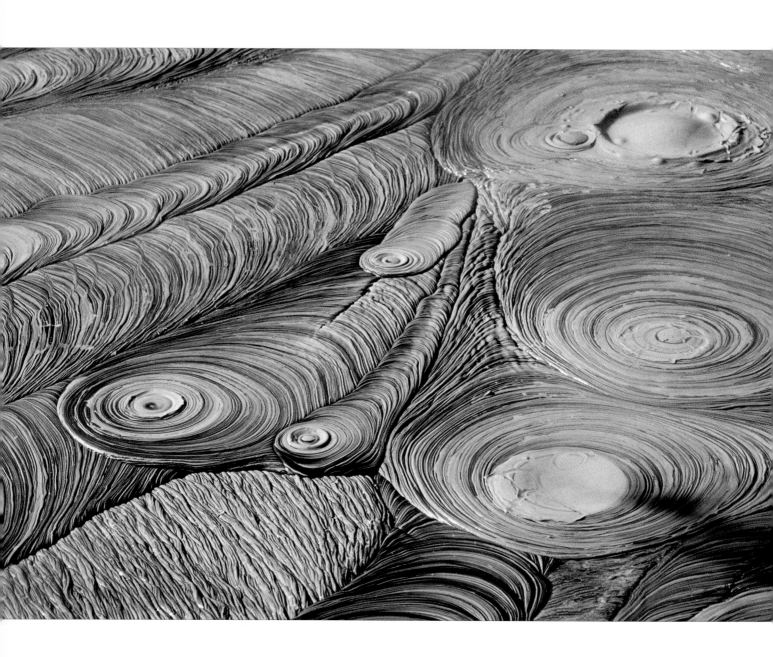

popular with surfers, the ideal way to visit Matakana is with someone who has a connection to the island. Alternatively, surfers can charter a fishing boat for the day. From the top of Mount Maunganui, it is possible to gaze across the water and see the expanse of the island in all its glory.

Further along the coast towards Whakatane is White Island (or Whakaari). This island is New Zealand's most active volcano; it is not unusual to see puffs of steam rising from the island. Formed by three separate volcanic cones, the dusty desolate landscape of White Island is like no other. White Island is now a Private Scenic Reserve; the diving in the area is superb. However, permits are required to land on the island. Boat charter companies run day-trips and diving trips. Alternatively, it is possible to view the island from a helicopter or from the mainland.

THIS PAGE (FROM TOP): *Visitors can enjoy a 'hands on' mud experience at Hell's Gate, one of Rotoura's most active geothermal parks; the smoke that billows from White Island, off the coast of the Bay of Plenty, signifies its status as New Zealand's most active volcano.*

OPPOSITE: *Boiling mud pools, geysers and huge, steaming craters can be seen in many places in Rotorua.*

a trip for the senses

A city on the southern shore of Lake Rotorua in the Bay of Plenty region, Rotorua is a fascinating destination. It is considered the spiritual home of the Maori, and the area was initially inhabited by them. However, after a railway was built and linked to Auckland, the town experienced rapid growth and the tourism industry soon began to take off.

Today, thermal activity is at the heart of much of Rotorua's tourist appeal; the bubbling mud pools, geysers, and steam rising from the ground are evidence of ancient volcanic activity simmering beneath the surface. A trip to Rotorua is not just a visual experience; it is an olfactory one as well. The scent of this remarkable natural phenomenon is pungent, and on a bad day, the aroma of sulphur can be overwhelming.

hot destinations

The locations where geothermal activity can be best seen and experienced are numerous. The Wai-O-Tapu Thermal Wonderland (a 20-minute drive south of the city centre) offers diverse sights such as multi-coloured mineral pools and the famous Lady Knox Geyser, which erupts on schedule daily, shooting water metres high into the air.

Hell's Gate is another popular destination. Located a 10-minute drive east of Rotorua, this reserve offers a strong cultural slant, and a splendid array of geothermal activities. In addition, the mud baths and mineral pools provide a wonderful way to relax, with the minerals from the water doing wonders for lingering aches and pains, and the mud leaving skin silky-smooth. Any extra pampering can be done at the Wai Ora Spa; they offer a host of treatments with carefully prepared products. Those interested in the soothing and healing properties of the water can head for the Polynesian Spa in the city centre. This Spa caters to all ages, with a family spa and freshwater pool for children, private pools and a scenic spa which overlooks the lake. Other often-visited destinations include the Waimangu Volcanic Valley, Orakei Korako Geyserland and Kuirau Park.

THIS PAGE: *Whakarewarewa is the most accessible and popular of Rotorua's thermal spots. The reserve is divided into two different parts; each gives visitors a taste of the vast scale of thermal activity.*

OPPOSITE (FROM TOP): *Rotorua is highly regarded in the mountain biking community for its tracks, which cover spectacular and varied terrain; with a well-established Maori community, Rotorua remains a cultural stronghold where visitors can enjoy performances such as the kapa haka.*

One of the most authentic cultural experiences is found at the Whakarewarewa Thermal Village. The village is populated by around 26 Maori families, and visitors will be able to see at first hand how geothermal activity is used for cooking, heating and bathing. However, the Whakarewarewa Thermal Village is very much a separate entity from what is now known as Te Puia, a thermal area that incorporates the New Zealand Maori Arts and Crafts Institute. Another cultural hotspot is the Tamaki Maori Village, a replica of a pre-European Maori village. Here, visitors are recommended to try a hangi, a feast prepared in the traditional Maori way, where food is cooked in earthern pits.

more than meets the eye

Rotorua is an area of outstanding beauty. The scenic attractions to be found there include the Whakarewarewa Forest Park (also known as the Redwoods) and the numerous beautiful lakes found in the vicinity. However, views of the spectacular volcanic Mount Tarawera, a volcanic mountain 24 km (15 miles) southeast of Rotorua, can only be seen through an organised tour, which will be by either four-wheel drive or by air. Mount Tarawera last erupted in 1886, a disaster destroying the Pink and White Terraces, and burying the Maori village of Te Wairoa.

Many of the activities on offer are centrally located; a number of water sports can be pursued on Lake Rotorua, such as fishing, windsurfing and kayaking. Rotorua is known for its mountain biking tracks, and the Whakarewarewa Forest offers superb trails. One of New Zealand's most exhilarating white water rafting routes operates at the nearby Kaituna River, with other activities like Zorbing, jet-boating and luging (a kind of tobogganing) also on offer in Rotorua.

Rotorua is home to the formal Government Gardens (close to the lakeshore on the eastern end of the city), and boasts several examples of interesting and historic architecture. Thus, Rotorua is a city famous not only for its fun-loving spirit, but also for its cultural legacy.

...the snow-capped volcanoes of the central volcanic plateau are a spectacular sight...

central plateau region

Although the North Island is best known for its beaches and summer activities, its widely disparate landscapes also offer scope for winter activities. As the weather starts to cool, visitors will make a slow but steady beeline for the Tongariro National Park, which offers superb winter sports opportunities. The Park is also well-known for its hiking route; the Tongariro Crossing is perhaps the best known one-day tramp in New Zealand. The three- to four-day Tongariro Northern Circuit is more demanding, but worth the effort. Both trails take in the magnificent lake and volcanic scenery.

snow season

Rising proudly from the plains, the snow-capped volcanoes of the central volcanic plateau—Ruapehu, Ngauruhoe and Tongariro—are a spectacular sight, which one can admire via the Volcanic Loop Highway. Mount Ruapehu boasts the award-winning Turoa and Whakapapa ski fields. Together, they make up the largest ski area in New Zealand, with 1,800 hectares (4,448 acres) of crisp white snow.

nature's hand

Volcanic activity has shaped the landscapes of this entire area, with Lake Taupo being the impressive result of a huge volcanic eruption that took place in 181 CE. The largest volcanic eruption for the past 5,000 years, it lasted several weeks and produced an eruption column 50 km (31 miles) high. Lake Taupo is today regarded as being the largest freshwater lake in Australasia. Taupo's proximity to the nearby ski fields of Ruapehu makes it an ideal base for day-trippers. Nevertheless, it is also a tourist attraction in its own right. Lake Taupo is an awe-inspiring sight, and the trout fishing inside the lake and its tributaries is believed to be among the best in the world. The surrounding lakes are also fed by numerous rivers and streams brimming with rainbow and brown trout. The Kaimanawa Forest Park boasts ancient beech forests, while the Pureora Forest Park is made up of untouched rainforests. Eco-tours

THIS PAGE: *Fishing enthusiasts flock to Taupo and the surrounding areas for trout fishing.*

OPPOSITE: *Central to the landscape of the North Island is the impressive sight of Mount Ruapehu, the tallest of the three active volcanos in the Tongariro National Park.*

are available at the Whirinaki rainforest. Wairakei Park, just outside Taupo, is home to the magnificent Huka Falls, a set of waterfalls on the Waikato River. The falls are a popular tourist attraction, and their sparkling water can be seen up close by jet-boat, or be admired from the land.

east coast

This region is located in the northeastern corner of the North Island, with small settlements dotted along the bays of the eastern shore. The population in this area stands at about 45,000, with almost three quarters of its people living in the city of Gisborne.

It was in this area that Captain Cook first landed on Kaiti Beach on 9 October, 1769. Famously naming the region Poverty Bay because he felt the area had little to offer. Cook couldn't have been more wrong, as local agriculture, farming and forestry industries soon became valuable assets to the region's economy. Although this region was the site of Cook's initial landing, European settlement in the area didn't really begin until 1831.

Gisborne can also lay claim to being the first city in the world to greet the sun each day, for it is both New Zealand's most easterly city, and the world's closest city to the International Date Line. However, as the New Zealand summer days grow longer due to the earth's tilt on its axis, Gisborne surrenders this title to the more hilly suburbs of Dunedin in the South Island.

The local wine production is significant (the Chardonnay is particularly good) and sunny days plus superb waves are a huge draw for surfers who flock to the beaches at Midway, Wainui and Makorori. Farming and horticulture industries thrive in this area, aided by the delightfully warm climate. The Te Urewera National Park is a popular location for fishing, hunting, tramping and horse riding. Within the park is the Lake Waikaremoana Track, a challenging hiking route. The native forest is a vast rugged area of densely forested ridges and valleys, unbroken save by rivers and lakes. Indeed, Gisborne is a city with much to offer.

THIS PAGE: The landmark Town Clock of Gisborne stands in the middle of Gladstone Road.

OPPOSITE: Horse riding has been initiated recently as a new venture in Gisborne, where treks lead over beaches and through native bush and farmland.

Te Urewera National Park is a popular location for fishing, hunting, tramping and horse riding.

hawke's bay

Hawke's Bay revels in its long hot summers and year-round temperate climes. A feast for all senses, the area is considered New Zealand's leading food and wine region. Hawke's Bay is the primary producer of the country's award-winning red wines, and is home to the nation's oldest wine-maker. A huge number of vineyards are packed into this relatively compact area, and the Wine Trail Map marks out the wineries that are open to the public for tasting at the cellar door. Many of these establishments have bistros and restaurants where guests are treated to delicious locally grown fresh food and niche regional produce, often in the very best al fresco setting.

sleek + stylish

There is far more to the region than just temptations of the palate. Napier is the port of Hawke's Bay, and is a city with a rich Maori and pioneer history. Completely redesigned after a devastating earthquake in 1931, Napier is known as the Art Deco city, with the style of its buildings reflecting the influence of icons such as Frank Lloyd Wright and the Chicago School. The National Tobacco Company Building in Ahuriri, the Daily Telegraph Building and Taradale's McDonald's 'McDeco' are some examples of the Art Deco buildings.

town + country

In addition to its elegant architecture, Napier holds further charms. The Norfolk Pine-fringed Marine Parade runs along the oceanfront. With views facing out towards Cape Kidnappers—renowned for its large breeding colony of Australasian Gannets—it is the perfect place for an evening stroll. Another scenic spot is the nearby Bluff Hill, which affords superb views of the area. Attractions include the Hawke's Bay Museum, the National Aquarium of New Zealand, and Marineland; also of interest are the Art and Craft Trail and the Antiques Trail. The surrounding countryside is used for horticulture, wine-making, and sheep farming.

THIS PAGE (FROM TOP): Napier is a fascinating example of a city that was rebuilt after a devastating natural disaster; residents of Napier celebrate the city's prominent architectural status with an annual Art Deco Weekend.

OPPOSITE: The Riverview Vineyard in Hawke's Bay lies by the Ngaruroro River, and is just one of the many picturesque wine-producing spots in the area.

architectural interest

Also heavily affected by the 1931 earthquake, the city of Hastings was rebuilt in an architectural style which combined a Spanish Mission theme with the favoured Art Deco design of the period. The Spanish Mission style had been imported from California in the United States. Buildings which reflect this particular style are the Dominion Restaurant, the Methodist Church and the Hawke's Bay Opera House. The pièce de résistance is the Westerman Building; it is a stunning structure, and a central feature of the city.

The views from the Te Mata Peak are superb.

The views from the Te Mata Peak are superb. According to Maori legend, the Te Mata hillscape is a sleeping giant, the hill being the body of the Maori chief, Te Mata O Rongokako. The fruit and grape growing and processing industry in the surrounding area make Hastings a prime spot for fresh produce, which is readily available at the traditional village farmers' market held weekly.

west coast

Taranaki is one of New Zealand's smallest regions, and it is named for the region's main geographical feature, Mount Taranaki (also known as Mount Egmont). A designated Surf Highway stretches along the coastline, offering enthusiasts an abundance of waves and a variety of surf experiences among the many reef, beach and point breaks. New Plymouth is the main centre of the region; it is a city known for its parks, gardens and nature reserves. Taranaki is also renowned for having some of the best public and private gardens in the country, and holds an annual Rhododendron and Garden Festival, which incorporates an exciting range of festive activities, demonstrations and garden exhibitions. The province is fertile, due to the generous rainfall and rich volcanic soil. As a result, farms dot the landscape. Taranaki is also home to the Maui gas field, which produces for most of New Zealand's gas supply.

THIS PAGE: Like Taranaki, the various stretches of coastline in New Zealand offer a host of different surfing challenges and opportunities.

OPPOSITE: Hang-gliding over the Heretaunga Plains in Hawke's Bay gives spectacular views of the vineyards below.

turbulent times

A number of fortified sites still remain in the area, legacies of the Taranaki Wars during the 1860–70s. This conflict ultimately resulted from the fact that the Taranaki Chiefs had not signed the Treaty of Waitangi of 1840. The fierce battles of this period have been documented in museums which preserve the history of both cultures.

mountain high

Located a little inland is Mount Taranaki, which provides an impressive backdrop to the waves breaking on the shore. At 2,518 m (8,261 ft), this near-perfect cone-shaped volcano is the North Island's second-highest mountain. The volcanic peak of Mount Taranaki dominates the countryside and is surrounded on three sides by the Tasman Sea. Today, the volcano is classified as dormant, having last erupted in 1775. In 1881, a circular area with a radius of 9.6 km (6 miles) extending from the summit was demarcated to be protected as a Forest Reserve. By the 19th century, more land was added to the Reserve and the area was gazetted to form the Egmont National Park, which is New Zealand's second-oldest National Park.

In winter, the mountain attracts ski enthusiasts. Come summer, trampers are drawn to the Taranaki Circuit, a three- to five–day hike which circumnavigates the mountain's base. In favourable conditions a hike to the summit and back can be achieved in six to eight hours. Both routes are noted for their breathtaking views.

wanganui region

Wanganui is a historic town with a riverside location. During the pre-European days, the area around the mouth of the Whanganui River had been the site of a major Maori settlement. Wanganui only began to grow in stature after the establishment of Wellington, when it swiftly became an important centre for trade. With the resultant influx of British settlers arriving in the country, Wanganui soon developed into a town.

The Whanganui River is New Zealand's longest navigable river and it is much loved by canoeists and jet-boaters. The river flows through not only the town, but also Whanganui National Park, which is one of the highlights of the area. The Park comprises a thick broadleaf podocarp forest with a variety of species of trees and ferns, birdlife, and abundant fish in the river.

THIS PAGE: Rapids, gorges, historic sites, farmland and forest scenery make a trip along Whanganui River, especially by canoeing, an all-encompassing experience.

OPPOSITE: An aerial view of Mount Taranaki shows off its distinctive conical form.

The volcanic peak of Mount Taranaki dominates the countryside...

THIS PAGE (FROM TOP): *The marae at the Te Papa Tongarewa museum. The museum is a centre for Maori culture, history and protocols; Lambton Quay is an attractive sight, both by day and evening.*

OPPOSITE: *The houses on the hillside of Oriental Bay encapsulate the stylish architecture of the capital city.*

windy wellington

The capital city of New Zealand, Wellington sits at the bottom of the North Island overlooking the Cook Strait. Aptly nicknamed 'Windy Wellington', Wellington is often buffeted by a blustery breeze due to its hilly terrain and fresh ocean air. The city is beautiful, its hillsides interspersed with an array of structures, ranging from grand colonial homes to ultra-modern glass and steel constructions. The views from the city and its suburbs are sensational, with some oceanfront locations offering views of the South Island and its northernmost Alps on a clear day.

a city for everyone

The city itself is a cosmopolitan, cultural hub with a cutting-edge arts community that embraces everything from music to film to fashion. Its close proximity to the Martinborough and Marlborough wine regions ensures that food and wine are high on the agenda, and the large number of restaurants, bars and cafés there are testament to that. Sports play a pivotal part in a Wellingtonian's lifestyle, and the Westpac Stadium—a leading venue for sport and concerts—is centrally located. Wellington is a very accessible city, with many attractions such as art galleries, the Museum of New Zealand Te Papa Tongarewa, New Zealand Archives, and the Beehive and Parliament Buildings, all within walking distance of each other. The New Zealand Symphony Orchestra, National Opera and the Royal New Zealand Ballet call Wellington home.

For shopping, the main retailers can be found on Lambton Quay; Old Bank Arcade is a haven of designer boutiques while Cuba Street is the place to look for the latest trends and retro must-haves. Wellington prides itself on its coffee; the streets are lined with fabulous cafés serving coffee that is second to none. For those who can stand the chilly wind, the harbourfront is a popular meeting place.

suburban retreats

An exploration of the suburban areas will showcase some of the city's finest features; parks, reserves and hilltop lookouts reveal lush green landscapes and fine native flora. The older suburbs such as Oriental Bay, Mount Victoria,

THIS PAGE: *Kapiti Island is a rugged, rural wilderness—the island is known for its untouched environment, which is carefully preserved by limiting the number of visitors.*

OPPOSITE: *One of the oldest and most popular tourist attractions of Wellington, the Cable Car provides a unique form of transport from the city to the suburb of Kelburn and the top of the Botanic Garden.*

PAGE 72: *Westhaven Marina, at the foot of Auckland Harbour Bridge, is one of the largest marinas in the Southern Hemisphere, and is home to many of the city's yachts and launches.*

Thorndon and Keldon boast some excellent examples of Victorian architecture. Stunning wooden hillside villas colour the landscapes, making Wellington one of the most attractive cities in the country.

The greenbelt areas, together with the abundance of accessible outdoor pursuits, make the capital a very 'liveable' city. One popular area is the Makara Peak park, which provides world-class mountain biking.

southern belle

Kapiti Island is located 5 km (3.1 miles) off the west coast north of Wellington; it is actually the summit of a submerged mountain range created millions of years ago. Once upon a time, the island would have been part of a land bridge that extended across to what is now the Cook Strait. A succession of pre-European Maori tribes used Kapiti for strategic and commercial purposes, or as a base for battles.

Kapiti Island has long been a protected reserve, and it is home to many bird species that are either rare or extinct on the mainland. Needless to say, it is highly popular with nature lovers. However, access to the island is limited, with only 50 people allowed on the island on any given day. Thus, forward planning is imperative for travellers.

country escapes

An hour's ride by car from Wellington, Greytown is a tiny village in the Wairarapa that makes for a great day-trip or weekend getaway from the city. With its original Victorian wooden architecture and rich history, it never fails to charm visitors. Further along the road is Martinborough, another extremely picturesque stopover. Originally a sheep station, Martinborough is now better known for its vineyards, and annual food and wine festival.

...making Wellington one of the most attractive cities in the country.

accolades boutique hotel

...a wholesome experience of Rotorua at its best.

THIS PAGE: *The outdoor decks are a treat for sightseers who will be greeted by scenic views.*

OPPOSITE (CLOCKWISE FROM TOP): *Relax outdoors with fine wine; scarlet sheets drape the soft, comfortable bed; billiards and chess are among the wide selection of indoor activities; enjoy al fresco dining on the expansive deck.*

On the edge of the beautiful Lake Rotorua sits the charming Accolades Boutique Hotel. Opened in 2006, this luxurious five-star lodge, with extensive views and landscaped grounds, is in a class of its very own.

The spacious design and floor-to-ceiling windows allow the dramatic beauty of the exterior to be relished at all times, while the plush furnishings create a warmth and cosiness that could only be discovered in an intimate setting such as this.

Indeed, the owners have thought of every possible way to ensure guests experience a relaxing stay. Soak in the breathtaking view of the natural landscape from the hotel's expansive outdoor decks. A billiard room, library and sauna, among other facilities, enticingly beckon one to unwind at the end of the day. The complimentary pre-dinner drinks and canapés only add to the feeling of being completely pampered. This attention to detail extends to the luxury rooms and panoramic suites. The flat-screen television with DVD and CD players, freshly ground coffee and English tea create a truly warm and homely ambience.

The rejuvenating spa treatment uses organic Pure Fiji toiletries—the very same gifts which Grammy and Academy Award winners have been indulged with for the past three years, and which guests can sample blissfully.

When it comes to mealtime at the Accolades Boutique Hotel, the legendary house fudge is just the tip of the iceberg. With some of the local ingredients fresh from the garden itself, guests will appreciate the exquisite homemade breakfast. And what better way is there to end the day than with a dining experience under the stars, featuring an international menu which includes local food specialities, complemented by New Zealand's finest wines.

ROOMS
2 suites • 6 deluxe rooms

FOOD
dining room • outdoor dining •
Continental breakfast buffet

DRINK
house bar featuring premium
New Zealand wines

FEATURES
high-speed Internet access • sauna •
library • billiards room • outdoor
viewing decks • spa

BUSINESS
conference facilities

NEARBY
Lake Rotorua • Lake Rotoiti thermal
pools • Hell's Gate Thermal Reserve •
shopping in Rotorua

CONTACTS
31 Flemington Place, Brunswick Park,
RD 4, Rotorua 3074 •
telephone: +64.7.345 5033 •
facsimile: +64.7.345 5066 •
email: stay@accolades.co.nz •
website: www.accolades.co.nz

Enthusiasts of local culture will be drawn to nearby Maori marae meeting places and the art and craft centres. Offering a plethora of pursuits from trout fishing and jet-boat tours to kayaking, sailing and helicopter rides, the surrounding areas of Lake Rotorua are also ideal for mountain biking, hiking and even bungee jumping, leaving adventure lovers spoilt for choice. While the dramatic landscape shaped by intense volcanic activity has created an adventurer's paradise, the region's geothermal springs have contributed to Rotorua's status as a haven for therapeutic mud spa treatments.

An exclusively intimate getaway to the Accolades Boutique Hotel promises to enthrall travellers with a wholesome experience of Rotorua at its best.

the boatshed

...a traditional island getaway...with a sophisticated edge.

THIS PAGE *(CLOCKWISE FROM ABOVE):*
*Classic teak steamers add
character to the louvre-
shuttered private deck;
a fireside chaise lounge, fine
cottons, cushions and throws
ensure a comfortable stay in
The Boatshed suite;
a nautical theme governs
The Boatshed's exterior.*

OPPOSITE *(CLOCKWISE FROM TOP):*
*Stimulate the mind outdoors by
the panoramic Hauraki Gulf;
the airy Lighthouse suite;
the use of space is enhanced
with an open concept, as seen
in this living and dining area.*

Just a 30-minute boat ride from downtown Auckland, on the quaint Waiheke Island, lies one of New Zealand's best kept secrets: The Boatshed. Overlooking white, sandy beaches and some of the most breathtaking seascapes, this boutique seaside hotel is a 'must' for travellers seeking a traditional island getaway but with a sophisticated edge.

While the sandy-toned, timber exterior of the hotel is reminiscent of seaside boatsheds from a bygone era, the interior embodies understated, contemporary elegance with a nautical theme. Independent from each other for maximum privacy, the seven designer suites' lofty ceilings and windows accentuate the spacious, modern feel, while details such as cosy throw rugs and an open fire create a homely ambience, where guests can relax in absolute comfort.

The Lighthouse is a three-storey hideaway suite with glass doors which open wide to the sundeck at the uppermost level. Here, guests may unwind with a glass of local, Waiheke-produced wine and view a panoply of yachts unfolding towards the edge of the Hauraki Gulf. For even more exclusivity, The Bridge sits on the other side of the property and features a private porch and an open fireplace. Opening soon on December 2007 are The Boatshed Bungalows. These two buildings offer greater privacy but with the same panoramic ocean views. Their rooms feature bathrooms which lead out to private terraces with open fires. Beach buffs need not think twice about a day on the white sand as beach gear, comprising umbrella shades, hats, sunscreen and towels are adequately provided.

Gourmet dining aficionados will be swept away by the mouth-watering delicacies prepared by the in-house chef at The Boatshed. The menus change on a daily basis and include succulent seafood or prime meat cuts, thrown together with organic, fresh vegetables

and served alongside popular New Zealand wines such as Sauvignon Blanc. Dinners may range from an intimate, candle-lit affair on a private terrace with the services of a personal waiter, a homely supper by the fire to a friendly get-together for a seafood feast in the hotel's stylish dining room. Come morning, sip a creation from the fresh fruit and vegetable juice bar before tucking into a continental and freshly cooked breakfast selection. Top the morning off with an al fresco café latte for a dazzling start to the day.

The range of massages, body rituals and spa treatments places the hotel in a league of its own. Body aches from swimming, surfing or sailing are best relieved by a Shiatsu massage or a Four-Handed Hot Stone Ritual combined with a designer body scrub. Such an emphasis on one's fitness and well-being is, indeed, the icing on the cake for this idyllic seaside retreat.

ROOMS
1 The Lighthouse Suite • 2 The Boatshed Bungalows • 1 The Bridge Suite • 3 The Boatshed Suites

FOOD
in-house chef • common or in-suite dining

DRINK
New Zealand wines

FEATURES
in-suite spa treatments • health spa facility • home theatre system • complimentary port and homemade dessert • minibar

BUSINESS
complimentary wireless high-speed Internet access

NEARBY
Oneroa shops • surfing • kayaking • coastal walks • classic boating

CONTACT
Crn Tawa and Huia Street, Little Oneroa, Waiheke 1081, Hauraki Gulf • telephone: +64.9.372 3242 • facsimile: +64.9.372 3262 • email: enquiries@boatshed.co.nz • website: www.boatshed.co.nz

the castle matakana

...the rows of yuccas and the majestic pair of phoenix palms...guard its entrance.

Beautiful country houses may be a common find in New Zealand, but that of a castle is surely hard to come by. Just an hour's drive north of Auckland, The Castle Matakana overlooks a country vista which frames Kawau Bay and its islands, Waiheke and the Hunua Ranges. Perched right in the heart of Matakana Coast Wine Country, the castle's 6 hectares (16 acres) of land include its own vineyard featuring a winsome 2002 vintage that is only available in-house.

Construction of The Castle Matakana began in 1984, and was completed in 1996 by Val and Ras Sutherland. Its design characteristics seem larger than life, from the tall Hollywood juniper trees that line the driveway to the rows of yuccas and the majestic pair of phoenix palms which guard its grand entrance.

Inside, a circular living room is endowed with a black leather couch, making the most of the minimalist fireplace and the surreal views behind it. Beyond its windows, the hills merge into one and the islands of Kawau Bay lie calmly in the distance.

There are only three spacious bedrooms in the castle, all of which feature breathtaking sea views and outdoor terraces. The epitome of luxury can be found in the Tower Suite, located at the top of a curved staircase, in its own turret. Like the living room, it is circular and elegant in black and white. And on a clear day, the view from here seems almost endless.

THIS PAGE (CLOCKWISE FROM TOP):
A circular reflection pool lies in front of the castle; the castle has elements of white Mediterranean villas; green pastures complement an al fresco meal.

OPPOSITE (CLOCKWISE FROM TOP):
Poached Pear with Rhubarb Dressing, an inviting dessert; large windows frame the views from the lounge; hues of black and white create a dramatic effect in the Tower Suite bedroom.

ROOMS
3 rooms

FOOD
dining room

DRINK
The Castle Matakana wine list

FEATURES
vineyard • pétanque • local artwork • bush • native birds • sheep

NEARBY
wineries • beaches • golf • fishing • Kawau Island

CONTACT
378 Whitmore Road,
Matakana, RD 6, Warkworth,
Rodney District, Auckland 0986 •
telephone: +64.9.422 9288 •
facsimile: +64.9.422 9289 •
email: mail@the-castle.co.nz •
website: www.the-castle.co.nz

Guests can spend the day playing pétanque in the castle's vineyard, enjoy a game of chess on the terrace, or simply laze in the sun on the ramparts. Nearby, the beaches of Tawharanui, Omaha, and Pakiri are ideal for laying an oversized beach towel and soaking up the sun.

Owner and artist Val Sutherland's work is on display throughout the castle, along with the works of other artists from New Zealand. Her artistic talents also extend to the kitchen, where she prepares meals which are fit for royalty. Breakfast, which can be enjoyed at whatever time guests roll out of bed, comes in the form of a banquet. Juice from the orchard's mandarin oranges, homemade granola with poached tamarillos, Deep Dish Blueberry French Toast with yoghurt and crème fraiche, and loaves of homebaked bread are served.

Lunch and dinner are by arrangement and guests receive exquisite menus, which are personally crafted by Val to complement the finest Matakana wines. Before dinner, guests are invited to enjoy a drink of local wine and hor d'oeuvres, wherever they choose to dine—within the castle or at one of the fine local restaurants a short drive away.

Close by are plenty of local attractions and activities for guests to wander through or take part in—wineries, art and farmers' markets, golf courses and aquatic adventures. The challenge, really, is leaving the comforts of The Castle Matakana itself.

delamore lodge

...a desire to unite with the unique surroundings.

THIS PAGE (CLOCKWISE FROM RIGHT):
*Walls made of handcrafted
curved plaster feature in the
grand courtyard decked out in
an earth-toned colour scheme;
rejuvenate the senses in the
tranquil setting of the warm
jacuzzi and sauna;
the outdoor dining area has a
massive fireplace and offers a
spectacular view of the
sparkling blue Pacific.*

OPPOSITE (FROM TOP): *Indulge in a
soothing bedroom ambience
in complete privacy;
the lush interior of the lounge
subtly combines the vast
horizon of the Gulf with
luxurious decadence.*

A recent star in the 'Hot List' of *Condé Nast Traveler*, Delamore Lodge is far more than just a luxurious retreat. It is located on Waiheke Island—one of the myriad islands to speckle the warm waters of the Hauraki Gulf—and moulded into a hillside mere kilometres from Auckland. The majestic wooden gates of the lodge invite guests to an exquisitely designed world unto itself, accessed via a captivating ferry journey across the Gulf.

With inspirations from the matau (a Maori bone fishhook) icon, the romance of the Mediterranean, and a desire to unite with the unique surroundings, homegrown architect Ron Stevenson along with the owner Roselyn Barnett-Storey designed this stunning lodge.

Each floor curves seamlessly into the next, in a natural replication of a cascading river-flow. Nothing jars in the colour scheme—sandy brown, stone and rich chocolate themes complement the verdant greens that abound outside. One reaches the library through a spiral stairway, with spacious lounges and dining areas nearby. The central courtyard boasts a cave-like jacuzzi, surrounded by a tropical rock pool and breathtaking waterfall.

For an island renowned for its vineyards and olive groves, local foods and wines are a speciality. Delamore Lodge even has its own well-stocked wine cellar. The phenomenal breakfast spread alone is a veritable feast of fresh pancakes and poached fruits, egg tartlets

and fresh pastries, to be enjoyed with a selection of remarkable gulf views. Executive Chef Tom Macguire's stylistic signature is absolute freshness, with locally caught seafood and ingredients from Delamore's own vegetable and herb gardens de rigueur. Pre-dinner drinks and hors d'oeuvres may precede an individually tailored four-course dinner at the lodge. A wide array of restaurants and cafés in nearby Oneroa or even Auckland, is also available.

After the evening's culinary excursion, Delamore Lodge's elegant suites await. Named Awatea (dawn), Motu (island), Mahana (warm) and Moana (ocean), each is north-facing for guests to relish the view at its best. The soft armchairs and king-size beds are the ultimate in escapism and first-class relaxation. Each hideaway has an exclusive private patio with superb views over Hauraki Gulf, ideal for sneaking off with a book, CD or DVD from the lodge's vast library. Saunas and a private star-lit shower provide guests with pure pleasure. Beauty treatments range from a classic Swedish massage to Lithos therapies, where incredible sensations are heightened with the use of heated and chilled rocks.

For outdoor activities during the day, golf, horseback riding and hiking trips can be easily arranged. The range of water sports includes sailing, diving, kayaking and fishing. Music lovers can look forward to attending a popular jazz festival which takes place on Waiheke island each Easter. Aerial enthusiasts, on the other hand, will welcome the thrill of a scenic flight or tandem paragliding. Indeed, the multi-faceted Delamore Lodge is the discerning traveller's choice.

ROOMS
4 suites

FOOD
tailor-made gourmet breakfasts • indoor and outdoor dining • complimentary pre-dinner drinks & canapés

FEATURES
panoramic views of Hauraki Gulf • private helipad • wheelchair-access rooms • indoor and outdoor fires • sauna • jacuzzi • CD, DVD and book library • award-winning wines • face and body beauty treatments and massage • vineyard and winery tours • horse riding • hiking • water sports • golf • airport meet-and-greet service

NEARBY
Church Bay Studio Gallery • shopping at Oneroa village • Waiheke Wine • Peninsula Estate • Kennedy Point Vineyard • Mudbrick Café

CONTACTS
83 Delamore Drive, PO Box 572, Waiheke Island 1041 • telephone: +64.9.372 7372 • facsimile: +64.9.372 7382 • email: reservations@delamorelodge.com • website: www.delamorelodge.com

heritage hotel + spa *du* vin

Hidden in the idyllic country valley of Mangatawhiri...

Heritage Hotel & Spa *du* Vin might be a mere 45-minute drive from the bustling city of Auckland but upon arrival, it becomes clear that this romantic retreat is in a world of its own. Hidden in the idyllic country valley of Mangatawhiri, which means 'river in the mist at the end of the trees' in Maori, it is one of those places where time seems to stand still.

The 16-hectare (40-acre) estate comprises 48 accommodation rooms surrounded by opulent gardens and the calming presence of nature. Unsurpassed privacy is only a closed door away, as inside the rooms are all the elements essential for those seeking a relaxing hibernation. Spacious bathrooms and well-appointed furnishings make for a cosy and intimate environment. Yet, guests who simply need to, can get connected to the rest of the world easily, as each room is equipped with a television, telephone and high-speed Internet access.

Hailed as one of New Zealand's finest spas, Heritage Spa *du* Vin's interior is designed with Balinese-inspired features—majestic statues of Buddha, hand-carved wooden bells and floating water lilies abound—to emanate a warm and enlightening ambience.

Offering some of the world's best treatments to help restore, awaken and heal, guests will be spoilt for choice with its wide array of packages. A good starter is the Executive De-Stress treatment, a purifying ritual that begins with an invigorating exfoliation using organic green tea

THIS PAGE (FROM TOP): Unwind by the scenic vineyards of Mangatawhiri valley; clear blue skies make for an ideal tour of the Firstland Vineyards; dine al fresco at the rustic Vineyard Restaurant.

OPPOSITE (CLOCKWISE FROM TOP): A Buddha statue welcomes guests in the Heritage Spa du Vin consultation room; the hotel entrance is flanked by well-trimmed greenery; board meetings are held in the executive room; the Spa's relaxation lounge.

and Dead Sea salt. A deeply detoxifying body mask is applied as guests slip into a light slumber. The pleasure intensifies with a full-body massage using aromatic and enlivening plant oils to stimulate lymphatic circulation and balance the entire body.

When it comes to dining, Vineyard Restaurant offers a seasonal menu of modern international cuisine by Head Chef Adrian Brett-Chinnery. Guests can either dine in the restaurant set next to the vineyard or out on the terrace. More private dining options are available in the Library, the Vintage or De Redciffe Rooms, and meals can be matched with a list of award-winning wine from the surrounding vines.

Within the property, there is also a wealth of facilities and services for guests who fancy a bit of activity, including a volleyball court, spa pools and tennis courts; as well as organised on-site activities such as claybird shooting, paintball and wine-tasting at the cellar door of Heritage Hotel & Spa *du* Vin's Firstland Vineyards. Away from the property, guests can indulge in a game of golf, guided walks in the Hunua ranges and horse riding. If one doesn't fancy golf or guided walks, then have a go at skydiving for a thrilling experience.

ROOMS
48 rooms

FOOD
Vineyard Restaurant: modern international

DRINK
Firstland Vineyards: extensive New World wine list

FEATURES
library • croquet • heated pool • pétanque • tennis • volleyball • fitness trail • mountain bikes • spa pools • archery • orienteering • team-building programmes • claybird shooting • paintball • skydiving • wedding planning service • wine-tasting

BUSINESS
business centre • conference facilities • executive boardroom

NEARBY
Hunua ranges • Auckland's Central Business District • Hamilton • golf

CONTACT
Lyons Road, Mangatawhiri Valley, RD 1, Pokeno 2471 • telephone: +64.9.233 6314 • facsimile: +64.9.233 6215 • email: res@heritagehotels.co.nz • website: www.heritagehotels.co.nz

huka lodge

THIS PAGE (CLOCKWISE FROM ABOVE):
Dine outdoors against
the picture-perfect
setting of Huka Falls;
the lodge blends
seamlessly into its
magnificent surroundings;
lush greenery enhances
the marvellous landscaping
of the pool area.

OPPOSITE (CLOCKWISE FROM TOP): The
beautiful grounds provide
a haven for the fauna;
the Owner's Cottage offers
entertainment in its cosy den;
enjoy stunning river
views from the guest suite;
a cathedral-style ceiling adorns
the en suite bathroom.

Huka Lodge has the honour of being consistently listed as one of the top retreats in the world, and it is not hard to see why. Located in Taupo, in central North Island, it is a property of magnificent natural beauty, and is set only 300 m (984 ft) upstream from the mighty Huka Falls.

With just 20 Lodge Rooms, exclusivity and privacy are the key notes for this six-star hideaway which continues to win prestigious awards year after year. Among its most recent stellar accolades are the awards for 'Best Hotel/Resort in Australia and New Zealand' (*Gallivanter's Guide*, The 2006 Gallivanter's Awards for Excellence) and 'Top New Zealand Property' (*Condé Nast Traveler*, Reader's Travel Awards 2006).

Each of the 20 Lodge Rooms is peacefully tucked away in the bush by the water's edge. Exuding understated elegance, the rooms are refreshingly spacious and boast bathrooms with every amenity as well as underfloor heating. Much admired are the wonderfully deep, made-for-two sunken tubs in the en suite bathrooms.

Families or friends travelling together can also check into the exclusive Owner's Cottage, which is in the grounds of Huka Lodge. Accommodating up to eight guests, this very private property sits on a promontory above the Waikato River and offers stunning views downstream to Huka Falls. All four suites have their own fireplace and come with super king-size beds, crisp cotton bedlinen and deep comfortable chairs for some serious lounging.

Outside, nature abounds. Charming ducks waddle about in the vast park-like gardens, oblivious to any human distractions. The lodge has a resident tomcat which has been known to spend the night with enamoured guests, prompting one writer to note, '[it made] the entire Huka Lodge experience not just six-star classy, but also six-star memorable.'

This focus on nature extends to the host of outdoor activities available at the lodge. Avid fishermen will adore the outstanding waters surrounding the property, which are rich with feisty rainbow trout. Five minutes away is the Wairakei International Golf Course, which has proved a firm favourite with Huka Lodge's guests. Over at Lake Taupo, indulge in aquatic activities ranging from sailing to jet-skiing. Within the lodge's idyllic grounds, guests can play tennis, croquet, pétanque or simply luxuriate in the waters of the splendid spa pools. For the ultimate side trip, hop on a helicopter and head to the nearby White Island active volcano.

Mealtimes are an exquisite affair with a five-course menu showcasing the freshest premium New Zealand produce, created by the lodge's acclaimed chef Twan Wijers. Guests can dine at the communal table or arrange to have their meal at a location of their choice—by the river bank, in the wine cellar, or at any number of deliberately romantic venues.

As a testament to the incomparable experience that it offers, Huka Lodge is often booked out well in advance, and plays host to many A-list guests with considerable discretion.

ROOMS
20 rooms • Owner's Cottage

FOOD
table d'hôte menu for indoor dining • outdoor dining

DRINK
wine cellar

FEATURES
tennis • pétanque • croquet • pool • spa pools • mountain bikes • massage • beauty treatments

NEARBY
Waikato River • Huka Falls • Lake Taupo • Wairakei International Golf Course • fishing • hunting • horse riding • four-wheel drives • helicopter flights • jet-boating • jet-skiing • kayaking • parasailing • bungee jumping • tandem skydiving • white water rafting • limousine tours

CONTACTS
Huka Falls Road, PO Box 95, Taupo 3351 • telephone: +64.7.378 5791 • facsimile: +64.7.378 0427 • email: reservations@hukalodge.co.nz • website: www.hukalodge.com

lodge at 199

...an exclusive lakeside luxury.

THIS PAGE (CLOCKWISE FROM RIGHT): *The private beach is ideal for soaking in the stunning views and a convenient starting point for kayaking enthusiasts; ebony-themed leather upholstery adds a modern touch to the sleek interior.*

OPPOSITE (FROM TOP): *The entry of the suite leads to an elegant dining room; luxurious bedding and idyllic views create a romantic setting in the bedroom.*

Situated by the shimmering shores of Lake Tarawera, Lodge at 199 is truly an exclusive lakeside luxury—at any one time, travellers who make bookings have the entire property to themselves. With a private chef, housekeepers and hosts at hand to cater to their every whim, the outstanding personalised service has made Lodge at 199 a part of the Panache New Zealand collection of exquisite properties.

In addition to a private beach and jetty, the five-star lodge also boasts sleek, spacious interiors, allowing guests to enjoy picturesque views from a haven of modern comfort. The leather sofas and polished wooden floors, along with original New Zealand artworks, make for a cosy yet contemporary setting.

All of the three extravagant suites provide seamless access to the deck, where one can enjoy a romantic candlelit dinner by the lake. Each room also offers the essential elements for entertainment—a flat-screen TV, DVD and CD players, and a vast library of movies and music. A highlight guaranteed to win over even the most demanding of guests is the complimentary house fudge, cookies and New Zealand chocolate.

Every minute detail has been taken care of, so that guests not only take great pleasure in having a memorable stay accented by warm hospitality, but also enjoy a distinctively 'Kiwi' experience. The impeccably landscaped grounds, for instance, feature a forest of native New Zealand flora, and tours offer an insight into the native plant species used in Maori cuisine. In fact, native herbs and Maori culinary influences are central to the dining experience at the lodge. Local seafood receives a new twist with karengo (seasoning made of seaweed) while venison takes on a distinctively Maori taste with ingredients from the Kawakawa tree, all aptly accompanied by an extensive New Zealand wine list.

If guests are able to tear themselves from these sublime pleasures, there is also a host of activities awaiting them in the magnificent countryside surrounding the lodge. Trout fishing and water sports are readily available on the lake itself, as are boat tours to Hot Water Beach, blessed with thermal pools in the sand. Be enlightened by visits to the renowned therapeutic mud spas and smoking geysers nearby. Of notable mention and immense appeal for any discerning traveller are the helicopter and seaplane rides—a breathtaking way to experience the natural landscape. The Lodge at 199 experience is an awe-inspiring one indeed.

ROOMS
3 luxury suites

FOOD
international menu with local flavour prepared by an in-house chef • seafood specialities • lakeside dining

DRINK
house bar • complimentary pre-dinner drinks and canapés

FEATURES
private beach and jetty • float plane service • helipad • high-speed Internet access • DVD and CD library • Maori culinary tours • kayaking • hiking • mountain biking • trout fishing

NEARBY
fishing and water sports at Lake Tarawera • boat tours • Maori heritage sites in Rotorua • geysers • Hot Water Beach • thermal pools • helicopter and sea plane tours

CONTACTS
199 Spencer Road, Lake Tarawera, Rotorua 3076 • telephone: +64.7.362 8122 • fascimile: +64.7.362 8255 • email: lodge@199.co.nz • website: www.199.co.nz

nicara lakeside lodge

...stunning views of Lake Rotorua...can be enjoyed from every room.

A new generation of New Zealand hostelries has emerged in which boutique five-star accommodation goes hand-in-hand with intimate levels of service. One such establishment is Nicara Lakeside Lodge. Set by the shores of Lake Rotorua, the lodge is owned by Heather and Mike Johnson. Who needs a guidebook with the Johnsons around? They have a wealth of experience and information on one of the country's most attractive regions.

With trout fishing as a popular activity in Rotorua, the four bedrooms of the lodge are each aptly named after a local trout fly such as 'Hughie's Mallard' and 'Tiger Ross'. Be mesmerised by the stunning views of Lake Rotorua which can be enjoyed from every room. The en suite bathroom features a beautiful timbered vanity and enhances comfort with its spacious shower and additional underfloor heating.

The focus on space and comfort in the lodge's bedrooms applies to the communal lounges as well. Rich rimu wood furnishing, a schist open fireplace and original artwork—pieces accumulated by the Johnsons over the years—not only add warmth to these relaxation areas but make excellent conversation starters. If the weather closes in, staying indoors will not be a bore, thanks to the lodge's fully equipped home theatre system and extensive library.

THIS PAGE (CLOCKWISE FROM ABOVE):
Lake Rotorua is a haven for avid fans of trout fishing; take a romantic stroll by the private beach at sunrise.

OPPOSITE (FROM TOP): *With an inviting presentation, the lodge's breakfasts never fail to whet one's appetite; the rooms offer panoramic lake views and lavish super king-size beds; a float plane awaits by the lodge's private jetty for scenic flights around Rotorua.*

Niicara Lakeside Lodge brings the concept of B&B to a whole new level. The Johnsons take great pride in the preparation and presentation of this most important meal of the day. The menu changes daily and every dish is accompanied by freshly brewed coffee or tea, hot toast with a selection of preserves, fresh seasonal fruits and homemade muesli and yoghurt. Depending on the weather, guests can tuck into breakfast in the dining room or al fresco on the vast deck, which overlooks the lake.

Customised itineraries allow guests to discover Rotorua as a hub of Maori cultural events and outdoor adventures, and as a thermal wonderland of geysers, mud pools and craters. Most of these attractions are only a 5-km (3-mile) drive away. Nicara is also a suitable central point for travellers who wish to embark on day trips further afield to destinations such as Waitomo Caves, Taupo, Hobbiton village (movie set for *Lord of the Rings*), Tauranga and the surf beaches near Whakatane. Or guests could take a helicopter flight from the expansive grounds to such locations as White Island, a captivating and accessible volcano.

Of notable mention is the lodge's sister establishment, the self-contained Nicara Lakeside Cottage. Located only four doors away, it is an ideal accommodation for accompanying guides, chauffeurs or caretakers. Just like the lodge, the cottage has a private beach and jetty, offering travellers unsurpassed privacy.

Not surprisingly, the lodge is recognised as a 'Five-Star Guest and Hosted Accommodation' while the cottage holds the title of a '4.5-Star Holiday Home', both graded by Tourism New Zealand's Qualmark. Truly, two superb properties in such close proximity.

ROOMS
lodge: 4 double or twin luxury rooms •
cottage: sleeps up to 6 persons

FOOD
homemade breakfast • indoor
or al fresco

FEATURES
private beach and jetty • home theatre
system • high-speed Internet access •
art collection • kayaking • fly-fishing

NEARBY
Rotorua City Centre • Agrodome •
Mitai Maori Concert • Zorb

CONTACTS
30–32 Ranginui Street,
Ngongotaha, Rotorua 3010 •
telephone: +64.7.357 2105 •
facsimile: +64.7.357 5385 •
email: info@nicaralodge.co.nz •
website: www.nicaralodge.co.nz

paihia beach resort + spa

Set against a backdrop of verdant mountains and overlooking pristine white beaches...

THIS PAGE (CLOCKWISE FROM ABOVE):
Each exclusively designed room
overlooks the Bay of Islands;
relax and unwind with
a generous view of
the Pacific Ocean;
the bedroom is decked out in
calming neutral tones.

OPPOSITE (CLOCKWISE FROM TOP): Every
piece of furniture exudes elegance;
fresh morning mist transcends
the outdoor spa pool area;
enjoy a poolside gourmet lunch
with a spectacular sea view;
couples will be enticed by the
luxurious massage therapies.

One of Captain James Cook's most celebrated discoveries, the Bay of Islands embraces the northernmost tip of North Island. A vast bay surrounded by 1,400 islands, this aquatic playground has become a favourite for visitors to New Zealand, not only because of the endless water sport possibilities, but also due to its breathtaking views.

Set against a backdrop of verdant mountains, and overlooking pristine white beaches, the five-star Paihia Beach Resort & Spa is a sanctuary of tranquillity. Every element of this stylish, award-winning retreat reflects the desire for guests to leave feeling renewed and entirely revitalised. With La Spa Naturale—voted as one of the Top Ten Spas in Australia and South Pacific by *Condé Nast Traveller (UK)*—in the grounds of the resort, this is guaranteed.

Guests will find it impossible to resist the spa's tantalising menu of massages, wraps, baths and scrubs which use local produce and clays. Succumb to a delectable Mocha Chino Mud Wrap, a Sugar Coffee Scrub or the custom-designed Milk & Honey Bath Soak in which New Zealand Manuka honey is used. Choose a 30-minute treatment for a brief respite or a five-day indulgence for that ultimate pampering. The treatments for women may be tailored differently from those for men, but they all promise to provide a rejuvenating experience. Guests can then relax and unwind in a private sauna or steam room before taking a dip in the 20-m (66-ft) heated saltwater pool and viewing the sunset over the sparkling waters of the bay.

The interiors of Paihia's suites are spacious and elegantly furnished, featuring floor-to-ceiling panoramic sea views. Showcasing a modern concept, they also come with DVD players, hi-fi systems and remote-controlled air-conditioning. After a day of exploring

surrounding islands in Missionhills on board, the resort's 22-m (72-ft) luxury motor launch, a quiet 'evening in' might just be what the doctor ordered. Light some aromatherapy candles and soak in a scented, 2-m (6-ft) spa bath for that much-desired rest and relaxation.

The unrivalled amenities at Paihia Beach Resort & Spa are further enhanced by its delectable cuisine. The poolside Pure Tastes Restaurant serves an award-winning menu, showcasing the best produce of the fertile soils and tropical climes of the Northland region, superbly prepared by Paihia's well-respected executive chef, Paul Jobin. Delight in the subtle flavours of the starter, Tempura Ludbrook Figs with Blue Cheese, Orange and Onion Purée, followed by the restaurant's signature dish, Thai Crispy Beef with Cucumber, Coconut Vinegar Relish and Coconut Milk Rice. Of course, a dazzling local wine should not be missed as an accompaniment to guests' meals. For a sweet finale, try the Dark Chocolate Tart with Espresso Gelato & Apple Chips.

For any modern-day Captain Cook who wishes to be enchanted by the Bay of Islands, Paihia Beach Resort & Spa can be found within a mere walking distance from Paihia Wharf—the perfect departure point to discover this treasure trove of holiday delights.

ROOMS
9 Deluxe Studios • 10 Superior Suites • 2 two-bedroom Executive Suites

FOOD
Pure Tastes Restaurant: Pacific Rim • indoor or poolside dining

DRINK
extensive wine list • cocktails

FEATURES
La Spa Naturale • ocean views • heated saltwater pool • Hi Fi system • DVD player • luxury motor launch

BUSINESS
conference room

NEARBY
Paihia Wharf • Kauri Cliffs Golf Course • Waitangi Treaty House • island drop-offs • sailing • parasailing • skydiving • kite surfing • scuba diving • big-game fishing • boat tours • dolphin watching • bushwalks • restaurants • shops

CONTACT
116 Marsden Road, PO Box 180, Paihia, Bay of Islands 0247 • telephone: +64.9.402 0111 • facsimile: +64.9.402 6026 • email: info@paihiabeach.co.nz • website: www.paihiabeach.co.nz

peppers martinborough hotel

...aged wooden floors, luxurious Persian rugs and fine china masterpieces.

THIS PAGE: *Soft lighting and flora fringe the open courtyard.*

OPPOSITE (CLOCKWISE FROM TOP): *Striking emerald coats the bedframe in a Heritage Verandah Room; the Garden Room has a more contemporary feel; a view of the library from the courtyard; lush furnishings and native hardwood floors grace the restaurant's spacious interior.*

Martinborough is a charming little village with a population of just 1,300. Situated in the Wairarapa region on New Zealand's North Island, it is home to over 30 vineyards, and is considered one of the country's finest wine destinations. Ask anyone about the best place to lay one's hat in Martinborough, and the answer is invariably Peppers Martinborough Hotel.

There is plenty that makes Peppers Martinborough a firm favourite among visitors, not least its fabulous location at the centre of the village, which places it within walking distance of most of the local vineyards. Built in 1882, the hotel retains its rich sense of history with its charming sloping floors and nostalgic artwork of local personalities on its walls.

With just 16 rooms, guests are guaranteed exclusivity. Ascend the hotel's grand flight of stairs and enter one of the nine Verandah Rooms. All of these open onto a deep balcony and exude their own distinct character with aged wooden floors, luxurious Persian rugs and fine china masterpieces. In the Heritage Verandah Rooms, old-fashioned claw-foot bathtubs add to the vintage charm.

The height of Pepper Martinborough Hotel's luxury is found in the Shek O Suite. In beige and blue, it features an elegant iron bedframe and steamer chairs on its own private verandah. It even connects to the Beetham room downstairs, if more space is needed. A more contemporary feel awaits in the Garden Rooms, which open onto the hotel's peaceful, leafy courtyard. Plump armchairs and sumptuous linen tempt guests to sink into their soft comforts and never leave.

Yet, to do so would be to miss out on the hotel's acclaimed Martinborough Restaurant and Bar. It serves a menu of regional cuisine, which is accompanied by an extensive range of wines produced

just beyond the hotel's doorstep. The restaurant's kitchen is headed by Chef Desmond Harris. His brand of modern and creative cuisine fuses classical French techniques with the freshest New Zealand produce. Savour the specialities, which include Natural Clevedon Rock Oysters with Green Apple and Chardonnay Vinegar Sorbet, and Crispy Free Range Pork Belly and Seared Scallops with Silken Tofu and Lemon Vincotto, among other mouth-watering creations.

As a testament to its popularity and warm and convivial atmosphere, the hotel's bar attracts many of Martinborough's locals. Pull up a chair at the grand antique oak table, or wind down by one of the wine barrels in front of the fireplace. The bar's collection of memorabilia and historic photos makes for great conversation starters, and engages guests in learning colourful stories about the village's history.

Reaching Peppers Martinborough is a cinch. Guests can drive 75 minutes east of Wellington or 3 hours south of Hawke's Bay. The Peppers Martinborough magic begins the moment guests arrive on its doorstep, with warm and attentive service that harks back to an era long gone. Indeed, the hotel certainly lives up to its reputation—coined by developer Edmund Buckeridge in 1882—as 'one of the finest hostelries ever erected.'

ROOMS
6 Verandah Rooms • 3 Heritage Verandah Rooms • 6 Garden Rooms • 1 Shek O Suite

FOOD
Martinborough Restaurant and Bar: contemporary French

DRINK
bar: extensive wine list

FEATURES
conservatory • pétanque

NEARBY
vineyard tours • vineyard bikes • tennis • golf • grass tennis courts • Aoteroa Stonehenge • wine-tasting • trout fishing • claybird shooting • horse riding • Cape Palliser seal nursery • Mount Bruce National Wildlife Centre • glow-worm caves • walking tracks • mountain biking

CONTACT
The Square, Martinborough 5711 • telephone: +64.6.306 9350 • facsimile: +64.6.306 9345 • email: martinborough@peppers.co.nz • website: www.martinboroughhotel.co.nz

peppers on the point

...extensive views over the sparkling waters of Lake Rotorua...

THIS PAGE (CLOCKWISE FROM RIGHT): *The Lake Villa terrace at night; relax in the Main Suite's spa bath with a mountainous view; the lounge room is remisniscent of colonial times.*

OPPOSITE (CLOCKWISE FROM TOP): *Enjoy breakfast on the terrace overlooking Mokoia Island; the Lake Cottage exterior; the Main Suite is generously proportioned, with calming neutral tones.*

What is particularly charming about Peppers on the Point is its rich history. Originally built in 1936, the two-storey mansion has been home to the Main family since 1974. Thirty years later, owners Jamie and Ron Main decided to open up their pleasant abode to discerning travellers in search of a peaceful base from which to explore the culture and geothermal wonders of Rotorua. The property's grounds span an area of 2.8 hectares (5 acres) to the edge of Lake Rotorua and the hotel's private beach.

Walk through its double wrought iron gates and it becomes apparent that this property is unlike any other in the area. Retaining its old charm and design, Peppers on the Point features a sweeping timber staircase and large entertainment areas with open fireplaces. History buffs will also be pleased to discover that many of the antiques on display provide useful insights into the mansion's past. In fact, the property is an eclectic mix of old and new, tastefully merged to provide a comfortable yet luxurious environment for guests.

The mansion comprises seven suites, of which each offers an en suite bathroom, complete with a shower, deep spa bath and underfloor heating. Most of the rooms boast extensive views over the sparkling waters of Lake Rotorua, stretching across to Mokoia Island and Rotorua's city centre. Two exclusive Lake Cottages are located just a few steps away from the main building; each offers an open-concept lounge and kitchen, and a large outdoor deck with a private jacuzzi. A new addition to the property is the Lake Villa, which sits higher up on the hill, directly behind the main mansion. This four-bedroom retreat is ideal for families or friends travelling together. A tennis court right beside the villa is an added plus for avid players.

Like any family home, the kitchen at Peppers on the Point is its very heart. From this magical room emerges cuisine worthy of any five-star international restaurant. The chef's passion for exquisite food made with high-quality natural ingredients is evident in every dish. Dinner is a four-course meal preceded by drinks in front of the fire, accompanied by a wide-ranging list of wine labels from New Zealand. Breakfasts are hearty affairs too, and include everything from Eggs Benedict to freshly baked pastries.

Most of Rotorua's attractions are within 10 minutes of the property. Guests can take in local history at Whakerawarewa, gasp at the geothermal springs, engage in a game of golf, hop on a helicopter ride, or spend a few lazy hours fishing for trout. For those seeking added indulgence, on-site massage therapy is the ultimate treat. Massages and wraps which make use of Rotorua's muds, minerals and natural botanicals are highly recommended.

ROOMS
1 Main Suite • 6 Lodge Suites • 2 Lake Cottage Suites • 1 Lake Villa

FOOD
in-house chef • table d'hôte dining • private dining room • al fresco

DRINK
wine cellar

FEATURES
tennis court • spa • gym • sauna • private beach and jetty • native bush walks • float plane pick-ups • DVD and CD library

NEARBY
geothermal sites • Maori cultural performances • golf • fly-fishing • fishing charters • forest walks • Rotorua Museum • helicopter flights • plane trips over active volcanoes • four-wheel drive expeditions

CONTACT
214 Kawaha Point Road, Rotorua 3010 • telephone: +64.7.348 4868 • facsimile: +64.7.348 1868 • email: onthepoint@peppers.co.nz • website: www.peppers.co.nz/on-the-point

skycity grand hotel

...designed by leading architects from the Pacific Rim...

THIS PAGE (FROM TOP): *The Grand Suite offers a striking view of the city from the 21st floor; a fusion of modern and oriental design pervades throughout the Luxury Twin room.*
OPPOSITE (FROM TOP): *Off-white furniture and dark-hued walls are a striking juxtaposition in the hotel lobby; at dine by Peter Gordon, marble, leather and timber sit comfortably with high-gloss plaster and halogen lighting.*

At the heart of New Zealand's most cosmopolitan city stands the SKYCITY Entertainment Complex, encompassing 17 restaurants and bars, a 'live' theatre, two casinos and Auckland's famed 328-m (1,076-ft) Sky Tower, the tallest tower in the Southern Hemisphere. Nestled alongside this entertainment mecca is the SKYCITY Grand Hotel, a beautifully appointed oasis of luxury, ideally sited in the vibrant city centre itself, close to the luscious vineyards, white sandy beaches and tranquil islands of Auckland's hinterland.

With a contemporary New Zealand theme, SKYCITY Grand Hotel was designed by leading architects from the Pacific Rim and is a pleasure to behold. Bold black columns, panelling and rugs contrast with golden marble floors and fabrics in hues of cream, bronze and taupe, to create an atmosphere of understated sophistication.

The sleek and modern design is carried into the rooms and suites, where clean lines, wood panels and frosted glass screens add to the sense of spaciousness. Spend a quiet evening in a hot tub filled with fragrant oils from the in-room spa products, before selecting from the wide array of in-house movies. Those who have to work after-hours can do so in style and comfort— a writing desk and ergonomic chair are standard fixtures in all rooms, as are dual-line phones and high-speed Internet access for guests' convenience.

If New Zealand's highest jump, the Sky Jump—a 192-m (630-ft) controlled fall down the Sky Tower—isn't exercise enough, guests should try the hotel gym. Packed with state-of-the-art equipment and supervised by fitness professionals, this ultra-modern facility also features a 25-m (82-ft) lap pool and jacuzzi for water lovers.

Alternatively, urbanites arriving from far afield will relish the opportunity to loosen up at the East Day Spa. Select from a menu of Asian-style massages, facials and exotic exfoliations to restore a sense of overall well-being, before embarking on an activity-filled holiday or business trip.

Perhaps the pièce de résistance of SKYCITY Grand Hotel is the gourmet dining. Peter Gordon, a highly respected pioneer of Pacific Rim fusion cuisine, has created a restaurant that will scintillate the senses as well as the palate. The enigmatically named restaurant, dine by Peter Gordon, has stylish interiors reminiscent of the Art Deco era, where dark leather arm chairs and curvaceous wooden seats are combined with exquisitely illuminated marble panels to set the scene for a memorable feast. The menu is complemented by New Zealand's most popular wines as well as vintages from boutique vineyards. Another good reason to stay at the five-star SKYCITY Grand Hotel...as if there were a need for one.

ROOMS
236 Luxury King rooms • 60 Luxury Twin rooms • 11 Executive Suites • 8 Premier Self-Contained Suites • 1 Grand Suite

FOOD
dine by Peter Gordon: international fusion • The Terrace Restaurant: à la carte breakfast buffet • SKYCITY Auckland: Bellota, Bar de Tapas y Vinos

DRINK
The Lobby Bar • Bar 3

FEATURES
separate bath and shower • in-room spa products • dual-line phone • data port • wheelchair-access rooms • East Day Spa • fitness centre • lap pool • sauna • Club Lounge (members only)

BUSINESS
SKYCITY Convention Centre • work stations • wireless high-speed Internet access • secretarial and courier services

NEARBY
SKYCITY Entertainment Complex: SKYCITY Theatre, Sky Tower, restaurants, cafés, bars, casinos, gift shop • museum • horse riding • mountain biking • Rangitoto Island • Waiheke Island wineries

CONTACT
90 Federal Street, PO Box 90643, Auckland 1010 • telephone: +64.9.363 7000 • facsimile: +64.9.363 7010 • email: reservations@skycitygrand.co.nz • website: www.skycitygrand.co.nz

solitaire lodge

...a veritable gallery of the finest native art...

THIS PAGE (FROM ABOVE): *Sited on a private peninsula, the lodge offers ultimate seclusion; the aromatic herb garden sits by the front terrace.*

OPPOSITE (CLOCKWISE FROM TOP): *The Tarawera Suite bathroom features double vanities and a double spa bath; a scenic mountain view from the Tarawera Suite; nature inspires the seat covers and sculptures in the lounge.*

Located on a private peninsula overlooking Lake Tarawera on the North Island, Solitaire Lodge certainly is in a world of its own. With only nine suites, exclusivity is a given and guests have the unspoilt natural surroundings all to themselves.

Refurbished in 2005 by notable New Zealand interior designer Mike Steiner, each of Solitaire Lodge's suites is positioned in such a way that the lake, lagoon and mountain panoramas are fully maximised for guests' viewing pleasure. This is facilitated by floor-to-ceiling windows, and private balconies which are perfect spots for outdoor dining as well.

The lodge's interior is largely decorated in earthy shades of cream, beige and brown and is furnished with five-star amenities. The two-storey Villa Suite is ideal for families while couples will enjoy a stay in the presidential Solitaire Suite, where a double spa bath awaits. Crabtree & Evelyn fans will be delighted to know that its products are offered in every bathroom. In addition, masterpieces by famous New Zealand artists—a veritable gallery of the finest native art—are on display throughout the property.

Over the years, Solitaire Lodge has earned a reputation for its amazing cuisine. Exquisite and innovative, the dishes showcase fresh New Zealand produce crafted in creative ways by the lodge's team of dedicated chefs. This fine cuisine is complemented by a list of wines chosen for their distinctive characteristics. The wine list displays labels from New Zealand's top wineries, all of which can be found in the lodge's extensive wine cellar. Dining venues range from the communal dining table which accommodates up to 20 guests, to private in-suite dining.

As a luxurious base, Solitaire Lodge offers charter vessels and float planes, ferrying guests across the area to explore nature's splendour. Enjoy a scenic cruise on the vast Lake Tarawera. Its crystal waters are fringed by native forest and sandy bays—the ideal setting for a myriad of exciting water activities. Lake Tarawera has also acquired a reputation for producing some of the largest rainbow trout in the Southern Hemisphere, and guests are often keen to try their hand at fly-fishing in the surrounding rivers and streams.

From the lodge's jetty, guests can also hop onto a float plane which will whisk them off to mystical Orakei Korako, or Maori for 'The Place of Adorning', widely regarded as one of the best thermal

regions in New Zealand. Along the way, the flight also covers the thermal hotspots of the Crater Lake District, Mount Tarawera Rift, Waimangu and Waiotapu. Upon reaching Orakei Korako, soak up the warmth of the thermal waters before taking off again on this adventure ride.

In addition, Solitaire Lodge liaises with an established helicopter service provider whose experienced pilots can take guests to the White Island volcano. Here, a moon-like landscape creates an almost surreal feeling. Powerful rumblings, however, serve as a firm reminder that the island is indeed an active volcano. Other tailored flights can also be arranged, including visits to local wineries, and transfers to and from any destination within the North Island.

ROOMS
6 executive suites • 3 premier suites

FOOD
dining room • al fresco on private balcony

DRINK
extensive New Zealand wine list

FEATURES
herb garden • spa • charter vessels • helicopter flights • fly-fishing • hiking • water-skiing • jet-skiing • mountain biking • kayaking • motorised dinghies • nature walks

NEARBY
Hot Water Beach • The Buried Village • Polynesian spa and massage • The New Zealand Maori Arts and Crafts Institute • white water rafting • golf • thermal reserves

CONTACT
Lake Tarawera, RD 5, Rotorua 3076 • telephone: +64.7.362 8208 • facsimile: +64.7.362 8445 • email: solitaire@solitairelodge.co.nz • website: www.solitairelodge.com

treetops lodge + wilderness estate

Sitting high in a small forest clearing, overlooking a volcanic basin...

THIS PAGE (FROM ABOVE): High ceilings, wooden beams and a full view of untouched forests define the conservatory; the bedroom opens onto a wide volcanic basin beneath.

OPPOSITE (FROM TOP RIGHT): The campfire-like setting makes the lodge ideal for intimate outdoor gatherings; the Great Room showcases ornamental objects which symbolise the essence of New Zealand culture.

In a hidden valley, beneath towering, rocky bluffs and amid 1,012 hectares (2,500 acres) of untamed, virgin forests stands Treetops Lodge & Wilderness Estate—a nature lover's dream hideaway. Located at the heart of the renowned geothermal region of Rotorua on the North Island, this secluded, ecological paradise is unique in too many ways to mention and is becoming a legend in its own right.

When owner John Sax decided to realise his life-long dream and make Treetops into what it is today, his mission was simple: to create a wilderness and game reserve that would be a testament to the timeless, rugged beauty of his native New Zealand.

Sitting high in a small forest clearing, overlooking a volcanic basin and surrounded by water, the lodge is built in the style of the early pioneers, using intricately carved wooden beams and local stone. With a 27-m (90-ft) long Great Room, games room and a library, it offers numerous cosy corners for sipping a cocktail and pondering the day's hunting, shooting or fishing.

Everything about the four suites and eight villas has been carefully contemplated to ensure absolute comfort—picture windows, open fireplaces in the living room and kitchenettes set them in a class of their own. Choose from a retreat nestled amidst the spiralling ferns and ancient trees of the forest, or an equally alluring villa with a lake view. Wallow in a steaming, spring-fed, mineral water spa bath after an afternoon's hiking and feel completely renewed. With attentive staff who are always there when needed but otherwise unobtrusive, the only thing missing to complete this verdant nirvana is unrivalled cuisine.

In keeping with Treetops' eco-friendly ethos, dining focusses on locally grown produce, which includes native Maori herbs to add a truly exotic twist to the menu. Savour the Roast Beef Fillet with Kawakawa Béarnaise, followed by a tiramisu with the buttery Kapiti Hokey Pokey Ice Cream, and a boutique New Zealand wine to end a perfect day.

Those lucky enough to visit Treetops can wander through 70 km (43 miles) of wildlife trails on foot, with a guide, or by horse riding and discover for themselves any one of seven crystal-clear, spring-fed streams, four lakes and an infinity of breathtaking waterfalls. This, in addition to the water buffalo, deer and teeming bird life that they might chance to see on their way.

ROOMS
4 suites • 8 villas • 1 cottage

FOOD
in-house chef • dining room or library

DRINK
extensive New Zealand wine list

FEATURES
spa bath • kitchenette • separate lounge • games room • library • conservatory • day room • massage • Maori forest food tours • guided four-wheel drive tours • GPS treasure hunt • guided photo safari • archery • bird watching • claybird shooting • fishing • hiking • hunting • horse riding • kayaking • mountain biking

BUSINESS
conference facilities

NEARBY
Rotorua geothermal hot springs • mud pools and geysers • Maori heritage tours • spas

CONTACT
351 Kearoa Road, RD 1, Horohoro, Rotorua 3077 • telephone: +64.7.333 2066 • facsimile: +64.7.333 2065 • email: info@treetops.co.nz • website: www.treetops.co.nz

waipoua lodge

...showcasing nature at its purest.

Established in 1890, Waipoua Lodge is nestled on a ridge overlooking one of the wonders of New Zealand's natural world, Waipoua Kauri Forest Sanctuary. It is home to Aotearoa's tallest kauri tree, 'Tane Mahuta'—one of the world's largest and most ancient trees (over 2,000 years old). Pristine beaches, turquoise lakes and 9,600 hectares (24,000 acres) of native forest all lie within easy reach of this beautifully restored five-star boutique lodge, showcasing nature at its purest. The lodge is easily accessible by a 3-hour drive on the highway from Auckland or a 30-minute flight to the private helipad.

Every care has been taken to ensure that the elegant interiors of this gracious and relaxed lodge enhance the original architecture, while historic memorabilia tell the stories of the region. Whilst sitting surrounded by contemporary art, polished wooden floors and leather furnishings, indulge in a cosiness accented by the glow of a log fire.

Housed in historic farm buildings, each of the four suites is uniquely designed. The Woolshed Suite offers deep china-blue furnishings juxtaposed against rich cream walls and 120-year-old kauri wood, while a passionate fuchsia theme prevails in the Calf Pen Suite. Alternatively, opt for more neutral tones such as those in the Stables Suite. Sumptuous bedlinen, plump couches and mohair blankets await guests upon arrival.

Dining at Waipoua Lodge is as natural as the lush environs. Locally sourced fare prepared by the private chef is complemented by seasonal and organic vegetables and native herbs. Some of these come from the lodge's gardens, creating a wholesome and delectable New Zealand menu.

The gardens stretch out from the lodge, leading to a forest walk. A hidden grove overlooks the regenerating forest, which is being expanded through eco restoration for future generations.

THIS PAGE (CLOCKWISE FROM ABOVE): Set amidst hectares of native flora, the lodge is a treat for nature lovers; visitors will be amazed by the view of the kauri tree by night.

OPPOSITE (CLOCKWISE FROM TOP): Enjoy a romantic walk along this idyllic bluff beach; a neutral colour scheme is used throughout the charming Stables Suite; discover bountiful flora in the Waipoua Walk; the classically styled lounge beckons with its warm fireplace.

ROOMS
4 suites

FOOD
private chef • organic cooking • common or in-suite dining • meals for children

DRINK
bar

FEATURES
helipad • wireless high-speed Internet access • sun-room with library • outdoor jacuzzi • trampoline and toys for children • mountain bikes • massage therapy • gift store

NEARBY
Waipoua forest tours • Trounson Kauri Park night walks • Kai Iwi Lakes • Hokianga harbour • golf at Baylys Beach • farm tours • fishing • four-wheel driving • snorkelling • diving • sand dune rides

CONTACTS
State Highway 12, RD 6, Dargaville 0376, Northland • telephone: +64.9.439 0422 • facsimile: +64.9.523 8081 • email: nicole@waipoualodge.co.nz • website: www.waipoualodge.co.nz

When embarking on action-packed itineraries, adventure enthusiasts need not miss out on the culinary delights of a picnic hamper comprising freshly made delicacies and a dazzling Chardonnay. Take a dip in the crystal-clear waters of Kai Iwi Lakes, or discover the seascapes of New Zealand's longest driveable golden beach, where one can also enjoy surfcast fishing. The majestic sand dunes of this region make for a thrilling board ride down their scenic slopes. 'Waiata' (sing) with the world-famous Maori forest guides, or join a night tour to view an extremely rare kiwi bird.

Nature truly is in balance in Waipoua. One of the few places in the world which is genuinely remote and tranquil, here is where travellers get to experience a peaceful sleep accompanied by the dulcet tones of the kiwi and tiny native owls.

the villa book

...a great help when planning that perfect getaway.

THIS PAGE (CLOCKWISE FROM ABOVE):
Fashionable décor defines this property on Waiheke Island; the spacious interior opens up fully to the outdoor deck; enjoy a view of Auckland's skyline and a direct access to the spa pool from the bedroom.

OPPOSITE (CLOCKWISE FROM TOP):
Dine al fresco by the fireplace and landscaped gardens; the stairs lead towards a private cove fringed by coastal flora.

With a growing number of luxury villas and apartments in some of the world's most sought-after destinations, it is becoming increasingly difficult to separate the excellent from the merely good. Hence, a reliable agency that can offer a shortlist of only the best and most suitable properties can be a great help when planning that perfect getaway. The Villa Book is one such agency, specialising in the rental of luxury villas and apartments across the world. In New Zealand, their impressive portfolio offers some of the most desirable properties in the country.

In Auckland, The Villa Book's apartment, set on the revitalised Prince's Wharf, is the ideal spot to kick back and unwind. Representing the very essence of waterfront living in New Zealand's capital city, the apartment offers dazzling views of Auckland's harbour and the city's North Shore. Each of its three bedrooms is superbly laid out in a palette of earth, white and cream. The entire apartment is literally wrapped around by floor-to-ceiling windows throughout. Thus, from any angle, the brilliant blues of the harbour and sky create a dramatic backdrop.

Most impressive is the apartment's 200-sq m (2,153-sq ft) outdoor terrace equipped with sunloungers, a private spa pool, cooking facilities and an evening cocktail area from which to enjoy a phenomenal sunset. By night, guests can gaze over the striking city skyline as they tuck

into a hearty dinner. The services of a full-time gourmet chef can be arranged, or guests can opt for a chef to prepare one-off meals. The apartment's fantastic location also makes it an excellent starting point from which to enjoy the best of Auckland, as trendy restaurants, bars and shopping spots are just a stone's throw away.

Just 35 minutes from Auckland lies Waiheke Island. Here, The Villa Book's property is similarly wrapped in a sea of blue, but instead of a harbour, it is surrounded by white sandy beaches and emerald vineyards. Sitting at the top of a cliff, this single-storey property has tri-folding doors which open on both sides of the living area to create the refreshing illusion of living both indoors and out. A large deck runs the entire length of the house and is blessed with sunlight throughout the day. From here, guests can take in beautiful views of the water and native bush. Should guests fancy a swim, the beach is only a stroll down through a garden of coastal foliage before the ocean beckons.

The property's three bedrooms also open onto decks and there is a spacious outdoor entertaining area to the south of the house. Here, all the accoutrements for dining al fresco—an outdoor fire, a large table and a barbeque pit—on balmy evenings await.

Indoors, amenities include satellite television, a DVD player and a laptop computer with high-speed Internet access. Culinary fans can cook up a storm in the property's fully equipped gourmet kitchen or request for an on-site chef. In addition, guests can opt for an in-house selection of New Zealand wines, as well as services such as private spa treatments and cruises.

Lakeside living is taken to a new level at The Villa Book's property by Lake Tarawera. Just a 20-minute drive away from Rotorua's city centre, the villa overlooks a natural lagoon and features a private garden, which leads down to a jetty. Take a plunge into the serene waters or enjoy a leisurely row on the property's boat. The three-bedroom property is brightened up by fresh, light colours and offers pristine views of the lake and beyond. Contemporary paintings and sculptures by New Zealand artists adorn the walls and provide eye-catching accents to the villa's décor. In the evenings, guests can dine al fresco with an unobstructed view of the lake. And with the kitchen well-stocked with gourmet goodies, guests are never left wanting for a snack or light meal throughout the day. Business services such as the provision of a laptop, high-speed Internet access and fax machine allow guests to keep abreast with developments at work.

Just outside the villa, nature beckons with activities such as fly-fishing and garden bush walks. Scenic tracks abound around the lake, including a 10-minute walk to the Cliff Road Reserve where a magnificent view of Mount Tarawera lies ahead. The surrounding area showcases a rich Maori heritage, offering much to do and see. Head over to Rotorua to explore the geothermal attractions and Maori culture, or wander through the forests and admire the exotic trees, a host of native birds and freshwater springs thronged with rainbow trout. The Villa Book can also arrange personalised trout fishing expeditions, which could well result in the freshest catch at the dinner table.

Trout fishing is also what Lake Taupo, with its crystal waters and natural volcanic formations, is most renowned for. Set right on the edge of the water is The Villa Book's elegant property, which presents breathtaking views of the lake from every room. Visitors to Lake Taupo, famed for its geothermal areas, can relax in its natural hot pools or visit Tongariro National

THIS PAGE: Watch the luxury launch pass by across Lake Tarawera from the comforts of the living room.

OPPOSITE (CLOCKWISE FROM TOP): Architecturally designed, this Lake Taupo property blends naturally into the landscape; an elegant en suite bathroom accompanies the master bedroom; with shutter controls, guests can soak in views of Lake Taupo one minute and return to privacy the next.

Park, popular for its mountain bike trails and ski areas. Just a five-minute drive away is the town of Taupo itself, where guests can find numerous cafés, restaurants, shops and golf courses in which to while their time away.

This stylish property, clad in sleek timber and with pristine white walls, offers two suites, each with an en suite bathroom, a walk-in wardrobe and kitchenette. Dual living spaces with their own fireplaces, underfloor heating, full kitchen and a spacious terrace allow guests private time away from each other if they wish. Otherwise, one living area can be converted into a third bedroom with two single futon beds. To best enjoy the surrounding view, guests can slide open the shutters and take a dip in the luxuriant pool for an hour or so. And if the romanticism of the occasion takes over, the shutters slide shut for privacy.

The Villa Book offers more options for such sophisticated lakeshore accommodation, which is located in both the North and South Islands. The experienced staff will be on hand to provide personal recommendations tailored to suit the interests of any potential traveller.

FEATURES
all types of accommodation to suit various needs • private chefs

BUSINESS
villa rental

CONTACT
The Villa Book, 12 Venetian House, 47 Warrington Crescent, London W9 1EJ • telephone: +44.845.500 2000 • facsimile: +44.845.500 2001 • email: info@thevillabook.com • website: www.thevillabook.com

clearwater cruises + helipro

...flat green plains turn into jagged snow-capped mountains in a matter of minutes.

THIS PAGE (CLOCKWISE FROM RIGHT):
Witness a breathtaking aerial view of White Island from the comfort of HELiPRO's aircraft; be it a cruise or helicopter flight, visitors will be in for a rare opportunity to savour up close the natural landscapes of New Zealand; cruise aboard the Clearwater Spirit for a romantic escapade.

OPPOSITE (CLOCKWISE FROM TOP):
Indulge in a private picnic at the summit of Mount Tarawera; take up jet-skiing for an adrenalin-filled holiday; the Hot Water Beach provides an idyllic setting for two.

It goes without saying that New Zealand's natural landscape is among the world's most stunning. It is also one of distinct contrasts, where flat green plains turn into jagged snow-capped mountains in a matter of minutes. The waters are a source of pride too, boasting rich, pristine rivers and lakes that are home to the country's famed trout.

To best experience the splendour of New Zealand's waters, step aboard a Clearwater Cruises luxury charter vessel. Endorsed by the country's official Qualmark licensing system and with a proven record for supplying an upmarket charter service in the Rotorua region, Clearwater Cruises has been hosting discerning travellers and corporate groups since 1992.

A favourite trip for many is the scenic cruise on Lake Tarawera. Its magnificent beauty aside, Lake Tarawera is renowned for its trout-rich and invigorating thermal waters. On these trips, everyone from the novice to the experienced angler can try their hand at fishing for trophy-size rainbow trout of up to 7 kg (15 lbs) using different methods—trolling, jigging, harling and fly-fishing. Once caught, the fish can be enjoyed sashimi-style or baked in the thermal sands of the nearby Hot Water Beach. While waiting for the natural oven to work its magic, enjoy soaking in the natural spa that is the surrounding thermal waters.

Clearwater Cruises offers three vessels of different sizes, accommodating up to 50 guests on the largest vessel, Clearwater Spirit. Guests can enjoy everything from fishing, water sports and scenic walks through native forests to unique dining experiences in secluded bays.

For those raring to take in the higher plains of New Zealand, however, there is really only one way to go: by helicopter. HELiPRO offers amazing scenic flights through New Zealand's raw and breathtaking scenery. From powerful volcanoes and thermal reserves, to the tranquil wilderness and dramatic fiords, visitors can whiz through it all while taking precious snapshots.

HELiPRO's excursions throughout the Rotorua and Bay of Plenty regions include walks across the active steaming crater floors of the renowned White Island volcano, or the opportunity to stand on top of the world on the summit of Mount Tarawera, the site of the largest eruption in New Zealand's living memory. Once flown to the sacred Mokoia Island, guests can also stroll among some of New Zealand's most endangered birds, or indulge in their own private slice of paradise by fishing at the serene lakes.

In the Wellington region, HELiPRO's flights encompass the spectacular Marlborough Sounds and wine-growing regions, as well the Nelson and Golden Bay areas. Just a 90-minute flight from Wellington is the Kaikoura area, famed for its whale watching opportunities.

HELiPRO's experienced pilots and their intimate knowledge of the local regions combine to create safe and insightful tours, making them the preferred operator for many of the region's luxury lodges and accommodation providers. Inter-lodge transfers and nation-wide touring programmes are also available.

Clearwater Cruises

PRODUCTS
charter vessels • skippered fishing boats

FEATURES
DVD and CD players • bathroom • bar • gallery • water-skiing • jet-skiing • tubing • wakeboarding • trout fishing

CONTACT
537 Spencer Road, RD 5,
Lake Tarawera, Rotorua 3076 •
telephone: +64.7.362 8590 •
facsimile: +64.7.362 8591 •
email: cruise@clearwater.co.nz •
website: www.clearwater.co.nz

Helipro

PRODUCTS
4- to 9-seater twin-engine helicopters

FEATURES
personalised charters • nation-wide transfers • flight training • jet-boating • volcano crater walks • heli-biking

CONTACT
Hemo Road, PO Box 291,
Te-Puia, Rotorua 3201 •
telephone: +64.7.357 2512 •
facsimile: +64.7.357 2502 •
email: rotorua@helipro.co.nz •
website: www.helipro.co.nz

south island

North Island

Cape Farewell
Farewell Spit
Stephens Island
Collingwood
Golden Bay
Abel Tasman National Park
Tasman Bay
Marlborough Sound
Motueka
1203
Karamea
Nelson
Picton
Keramea Bight
Richmond
Havelock
Cook Strait
1875
Blenheim

Tasman Sea

Westport
Murchison
St. Arnaud
> The Lodge at Paratiho Farms
> Hapuku Lodge
> Kincaid Lodge

2339
2885
Tapuaenuku
Punakaiki
Reefton
2160
Manakau

Greymouth
Hanmer Spring
Kaikoura
Lake Brunner
Lewis Pass
Kaikoura Peninsula

Hokitika
Arthur's Pass
2400

Whataroa
2795
Pegasus Bay
> Sherwood Lodge
Franz Josef Glacier
Southern Alps
> Claremont Country Estate
Fox Glacier
3764
> Hotel Off The Square
Mt. Cook
Christchurch
> Huntley House
Mount Cook Village
Lyttelton
Banks Peninsula
Haast
Lake Tekapo
Ashburton
Akaora
> The Villa Book
> Millbrook
Lake Pukaki
Canterbury Bight
> The Spire Queenstown
Haast Pass
Temuka

Mt. Aspiring 3027
Twizel
Timaru
1910
Lake Hawea
Milford Sound
2746
Lake Wanaka
Milford Sound
Mt. Tutoko
Wanaka
2134
Glenorchy
Waimate
> Cardrona Terrace Estate
> Matakauri Lodge
2131
Arrowtown
> Browns Sotheby's International Realty
> Blanket Bay
Cromwell
Oamaru
> Eichardt's Private Hotel
> Takaro
Lake Wakatipu
> Glacier Southern Lakes Helicopters
Doubtful Sound
2324 The Remarkables
> The Villa Book
Queenstown
Alexandra
Lake Te Anau
1450
Resolution Island
1853
Palmerston
Lake Manapouri
Te Anau
Dusky Sound
Manapouri
Lumsden
Otago Peninsula
Dunedin
1189
Gore
Winton
Milton
Balclutha
Invercargill
Bluff
Catlins Conservation Park
Solander Island
Chasland Mistake
Codfish Island
980
Ruapuke Island
Oban
Halfmoon Bay
South Pacific Ocean
Stewart Island
Mutton Bird Islands
South Cape

Foveaux Strait

N

Legend
≡ Highway
■ Main Road
⊕ Airport
Water
● 3000–4000 m
● 2000–3000 m
● 1000–2000 m
● 500–1000 m
● 200–500 m

0 km   60   120   180 km

south island

The South Island is a nature lover's playground of forests, lakes, glaciers and mountains. If variety is one's spice of life, then visitors will never be bored on the South Island, such is its charm of ever-changing scenery. The Southern Alps reign majestically over the landscape, dividing the island in two. The northern region is characterised by the waterways, islets and golden sands of the coastline.

More recently the area has become the hub of an internationally successful wine industry, with acres of vineyards basking in the sunshine beneath the shadows of the mountains. The Canterbury region is known for its sweeping plains, and the farmland areas of Otago and Southland are scattered with sheep and cattle. Amidst the splendour of the natural environment, the historical significance of cities such as Christchurch and Dunedin pose an interesting distraction, but when set against the unworldly magnificence of Fiordland, seem almost incongruous. Rich with wildlife, the South Island offers a never-ending array of delights.

marlborough region

The Marlborough region of the South Island is packed with a diverse range of experiences. Among them are the waterways of Marlborough Sounds and whale watching opportunities. At the tip of the South Island nestles the portside town of Picton. The gateway to the beauty that lies beyond, Picton is a great launch pad to Marlborough Sounds. It is also the access point to the spectacular Queen Charlotte Track, a four-day, 67-km (42-mile) tramp offering stunning coastal and bush scenic views of the Marlborough Sounds. The vista can also be enjoyed from the comfort of a car along the Queen Charlotte drive; this scenic road stretches from Havelock and ends in Picton. It is one of the most stunning road trips in the country.

PAGE 110: *A colony of Takapu (Australasian Gannets) in Dunedin dot the landscape as far as the eye can see.*

THIS PAGE: *The poppy fields of Blenheim create a stunning splash of colour across the countryside.*

OPPOSITE: *Lake Matheson has in its waters the reflection of one of the country's most famous views: the snow-capped peaks of Aoraki/Mount Cook and Tasman.*

untamed beauty

Flanked by verdant bush-clad hills, Marlborough Sounds are a maze of deep coves, secluded bays and sheltered waterways. The Sounds encompass Port Underwood, Queen Charlotte Sound, Pelorus and Kenepuru Sounds. There are a number of water activities on offer: diving, sailing and kayaking among them. Designated picnic and camping spots can be found at various bays; this is an area that begs to be explored in a leisurely fashion. Renowned for its fabulous vineyards, Blenheim's herbaceous Sauvignon Blanc wines are recognised internationally. The Wairau valley is home to a number of wineries all concentrated within a small area, thus making a wine tour easy to navigate.

marine parade

With snow-capped mountains as a backdrop, Kaikoura (Maori for a 'meal of crayfish') is a small seaside town midway between Picton and Christchurch. Located on the rugged east coast, it is best known for the startling abundance of marine life found off its Peninsula.

ABOVE: Picton is the first port of call for visitors crossing from the North Island by ferry. The base for cruising the Marlborough Sounds, it has stunning views of forested mountains rising from the sea.

OPPOSITE: Sperm whales can be seen in abundance off the shores of Kaikoura; sightings are reported to be most frequent between October and August.

Maori tribes were attracted to settle here by the wealth of sea fare. According to Maori legend, the demigod Maui placed his foot on the Kaikoura Peninsula to steady himself when he 'fished up' the North Island. The strong Maori legacy is still evident today, both physically and spiritually. In the mid-1800s, Kaikoura developed as a centre for the whale industry. However, as the numbers of whales declined, other industries were sought. Today, the emphasis is now very much on conservation.

whale spotting

There are few experiences as awe-inspiring as seeing a whale in close proximity, and Kaikoura offers exceptional opportunities to spot these magnificent mammals. A variety of species can be seen off Kaikoura at different times of the year. The huge Sperm Whales are the most frequent guests. Less frequent but still sighted are Humpback Whales, Pilot Whales, Blue Whales and Southern Right Whales. New Zealand Fur Seals are commonly observed basking off the rocks, and pods of Dusky Dolphins are

found in abundance, frolicking in the ocean and playing tag with passing sea vessels. Various tour operators in the area offer every kind of marine experience. However, in order to limit the number of boats trying to sight whales, there are only four companies which have permits to guide tourists out to see the whales at close quarters.

nelson region

Surrounded by mountain ranges, the Nelson Tasman region gazes out over Tasman Bay towards snow-capped mountains. Within the region are three national parks: Nelson Lakes, Kahurangi and Abel Tasman. Nelson is New Zealand's second-oldest city, its name derived from Admiral Nelson, the commander of the British fleet which emerged victorious at the Battle of Trafalgar in 1805. In fact, many landmarks and roads within the city have been named after the people and ships associated with that battle. This city's tranquil ambience will attract visitors who are eager to explore its hub and surrounding area. Lush green tree-lined streets and historical shop façades denote the main thoroughfare of Trafalgar Street. At the top of the street, the Christ Church Cathedral surveys the city from its hilltop vantage point. This impressive structure dominates the landscape; its curious mix of architectural styles marks the prolonged period of its construction.

The region is an art-focused one—there are umpteen galleries and craft centres to be found not only in the city, but in the surrounding area as well. The Suter Art Gallery is one of New Zealand's oldest galleries, and holds an impressive collection of works. The city also hosts popular annual events such as the Nelson Arts Festival and the Jazz Festival, the former consisting of arts events and activities spanning over a week. Nelson is also renowned for the freshness of its seafood. Home to fabulous restaurants and eateries, it offers dining opportunities of a high calibre, both in the city area and the surrounding neighbourhoods.

THIS PAGE (FROM TOP): Revellers dressed to the hilt during a parade at the annually held Nelson Arts Festival; in an area known for its fine seafood, most visitors will feel compelled to sample the local fare on offer, such as this Salman Fillet with Berries and Currants meal.

OPPOSITE: Framed by snow-capped mountains on the horizon, sunrise in Kaikoura is a glorious affair.

...the Nelson Tasman region gazes out over Tasman Bay towards snow-capped mountains.

The Abel Tasman National Park is famous for its sparkling ocean...

walkers' paradise

Many people travel to this region to relish its exemplary countryside. Nelson is a walkers' paradise with over 40 different tracks within a 16 km (10 mile) radius of the city. The Mount Richmond Forest Park provides a lush backdrop to Nelson city, with its dense forest delighting trampers. The Nelson Lakes National Park lies about 80 km (50 miles) southwest from Nelson. Two glacial lakes—Rotoiti and Rotoroa—are edged by forest and a mountainous backdrop. Described as a 'winter wonderland', the area is popular for skiing in the cold season, and other outdoor pursuits. Kahurangi National Park is a magnet for trampers, as a number of trails run through it. Particularly well-known is the Heaphy Track, although it is the other more arduous and isolated trails that attract dedicated walkers.

nature's riches

The Abel Tasman National Park is famous for its beaches the colour of liquid gold, the sparkling ocean with hues that range from aquamarine to emerald to Indian ink, and its hectares of lush native forest. A water-fringed playground of hiking trails, kayaking trips and sailing excursions, its domain also encompasses areas of historical merit as well as beauty.

The Park was created in December 1942. It was named after the Dutch explorer Abel Janszoon Tasman, who had sailed into Golden Bay at the northern tip of the park in 1642. The Maori people had long lived along the Abel Tasman coast, but with European settlement and the resultant steady increase in logging and mining of granite, the landscape began to suffer. Ultimately, local campaigning led to the creation of the Abel Tasman National Park.

Within the Park, the Abel Tasman Coastal Track is one of New Zealand's Great Walks, and is among the most beautiful in the country. It is possible to combine activities (for example, walking with kayaking), or to take a sightseeing boat tour. A host of tour operators offer various options for the discerning traveller. Many trips leave from Kaiteriteri or Marahau, although it is possible to take a bus transfer from Nelson, which is only about an hour-and-a-half's drive away.

THIS PAGE: *The waterscapes along the South Island coastline are truly breathtaking.*

OPPOSITE: *Located in the Abel Tasman National Park, the Split Apple Rock is best viewed from the water; at close quarters, it presents an impressive sight.*

beautiful beaches

Golden Bay can be accessed via the Takaka Hill Road, where the scenery is dramatic. The area takes in a number of small towns and resorts. However, it is largely synonymous with the long stretch of beach that leads up to Farewell Spit. From the sand dunes, the views are spectacular.

canterbury region

This is an area of distinctive landscapes, with the snow-peaked Southern Alps posing as a backdrop for the expanses of flat plains, rivers and beaches below. Christchurch lies in Canterbury between the Banks Peninsula and the Canterbury Plains. Called the 'Garden City', Christchurch is the oldest city in New Zealand, and is notably English in style, with its harmonious collection of mostly Victorian buildings. Panoramic views of the city can be obtained from almost any high-rise building, as much of the cityscape is flat and rises only a few metres above sea level.

Lush and picturesque, Christchurch is famous for its Botanic Gardens, which cover an impressive 30 hectares (74 acres) largely within the loop of the Avon River. The Gardens were established in 1863 by pioneering British settlers who brought with them their gardening traditions. Since then, a fabulous collection of exotic and indigenous plants has been cultivated; these are displayed in greenhouses, thematic gardens and on lawns. There are also numerous large majestic trees that provide a perfect backdrop to the Gardens' sweeping lawns and plant collections.

The main focal point of the city centre is its magnificent Cathedral, which overlooks the paved Cathedral Square; its spire reaches 63 m (207 ft) above ground level, thus providing great views over the centre of the city. Designed in the gothic revival style by the prominent English architect Sir George G. Scott, the Cathedral took exactly 40 years (1864–1904) to construct. The square is an ideal venue for performers, artisans, craft stalls and food stands.

THIS PAGE (FROM TOP):
The Christchurch Cathedral is pivotal to the history of the city. One can climb the 133 steps up to its spire for a bird's eye view across the city; the Golden Bay beach.
OPPOSITE: The Flower Clock in Victoria Square, Christchurch.

Called the 'Garden City', Christchurch is the oldest city in New Zealand...

city of culture

The cultural focus of the city remains very important, and the Arts Centre, Art Gallery, Centre of Contemporary Art and the Canterbury Museum all form a part of the 'Cultural Precinct' concept in the central area. This unique cultural heart of Canterbury incorporates education, art, religion and recreational activities, all within an area of less than 1 sq km (0.4 sq mile) enclosed by the Avon River. Easily navigated on foot or by bicycle, the city is a delight to explore. The old tramway has been restored and trams now operate a tour around central Christchurch, meandering past key sights. Christchurch is also considered a great sports centre, and the city boasts Jade Stadium, the largest stadium on the South Island. This ground is used all year round to host rugby and cricket matches.

wider realms

With a myriad of attractions within its environment, Christchurch is establishing itself as a city for all seasons and a gateway to the beautiful Canterbury region, where there is much to be discovered. To the north, through Amberley, the relatively-new wine-growing area of Waipara is rapidly developing. Further north is Hanmer Springs. Best known for its thermal reserves, the hot pools are surrounded by a forest park which offers a range of activities.

A central Canterbury highlight is the Arthur's Pass National Park. Sharing the same name as a spectacular highway that crosses the Southern Alps, this road traverses monumental scenery. The park is known for its beautiful fields of alpine flowers, native forests and wild mountains. Other distinctive attributes of the area are the many glaciers retained from the ice ages. The southern part of the Canterbury region incorporates the mighty Aoraki/Mount Cook National Park.

THIS PAGE (FROM TOP): Regent Street is an idyllic area to relax and enjoy al fresco dining; the Christchurch tram takes in many of the main tourist attractions, such as the Christchurch Art Gallery. Passengers can hop on and off trams at their leisure.

OPPOSITE: The pristine snow of the glaciers of the Southern Alps provide a spectacular sight for locals and tourists alike.

frozen glory

Amidst the vast sheep-peppered plains, emerald-green valleys and turquoise-blue lakes of Mackenzie Country towers Aoraki/Mount Cook. At 3,754 m (12,316 ft), Mount Cook is easily Australasia's tallest mountain, towering over even the Southern Alps. This is an area of legend for both the Maori and Europeans. The Maori story tells the tale of a young boy, Aoraki, and his three brothers who were travelling in a canoe when they were struck by disaster. Frozen by the wind, they turned into stone. Aoraki is now known as Aoraki/Mount Cook and the Southern Alps, his brothers. The European legend is less glamorous—the region was named after one of New Zealand's most famous outlaws, James McKenzie, a sheep rustler whose escapades brought him notoriety.

There are a multitude of walks and hikes in the vicinity of Mount Cook, which can last from half an hour to several days. An alternative option is a Heli or scenic flight; the glacier landings give spectacular views of the Southern Alps and the vast snowfields below. Accommodation is readily available at the alpine village of Mount Cook, and the airport is a short distance away.

west coast region

The West Coast is a wild, rugged region, and while there are a number of attractions, Fox and Franz Josef Glaciers are considered the jewels in the crown. Relics from the last ice age, these glaciers are 20 km (12.4 miles) apart, and both cut through glacial valleys to flow into temperate rainforest. Close to each glacier is a small township with accommodation and restaurants. It is possible to see the glaciers by air or on foot. Short valley walks or glacier walking (guided walks on the ice) reveal incredible landscapes. The steep icefalls that are mazes of crevasses and pinnacles of ice make for spectacular viewing. Indeed, to see at first hand the pure blue colour of ice is a truly startling visual experience. Lake Matheson is close by, which when caught in the right conditions, provides a picture-perfect moment—it can reflect an almost mirror image of Aoraki/Mount Cook in its waters.

If you are an adrenalin lover, Queenstown is the ultimate destination to head for.

otago region

The Otago region will satisfy culture vultures, adventure seekers and epicureans alike. The city of Dunedin is a historical stronghold; the gold-mining townships of central Otago are also reminders of a previous era. A growing wine industry thrives in this area. If you are an adrenalin lover, Queenstown is the ultimate destination to head for.

The name Dunedin is derived from the Gaelic form of Edinburgh. In 1846, Charles Kettle, a British land surveyor, was vested with the responsibility of planning a new town; his instructions were to incorporate features of Edinburgh. The strong character of its founding inspiration became a notable feature in the city. For a time Dunedin was the largest and wealthiest city in New Zealand after the discovery of gold in the Otago region in 1861. The buildings and architecture that sprung up reflected this wealth. Today, Dunedin is considered the most well-preserved town of Victorian and Edwardian heritage in the Southern Hemisphere.

glorious foundations

Among the buildings worthy of mention is the Dunedin Railway Station. Opened in 1906, the Flemish Renaissance-style building is an outstanding structure. The Municipal Chambers date back from 1880, and reflect the wealth of the period; the similarly dated University of Otago clock tower is another famous landmark. Venture 15 minutes from the city and discover the Larnach Castle. This impressive residence is surrounded by fabulous formal gardens.

During the 1980s the city's popular music scene blossomed, with many local bands such as The Chills and The Verlaines gaining national and international recognition. Present-day Dunedin is also renowned for being a 'university city', its thriving tertiary student population supporting a vibrant youth culture, and a continuation of the musical scene which their generation grew up with. This, when combined with a very strong visual arts community that also lives in Dunedin, has led to a burgeoning café culture and buzzing bar scene, thus helping to establish the city as a hip and lively hangout.

THIS PAGE: *The Dunedin Railway Station is an iconic feature of this historic city. Major restoration work was undertaken in 1999 to return the station to its full glory.*

OPPOSITE: *An aerial view reveals spectacular views of Queenstown and the mountains behind it.*

wildlife enthusiasts

Within easy access to the city is the Otago Peninsula. Home to rare and unusual wildlife, the world's only mainland albatross-breeding colony can be found at Taiaroa Head. In addition, various other ocean bird, seal and penguin species—including one of the world's rarest (the Yellow-Eyed Penguin)—can all be found here.

action stations

Vibrant and cosmopolitan, Queenstown is armed with a reputation for being the adventure capital of the world. Indeed, the activities of Queenstown are not for the faint-hearted. Whether it is skydiving, bungee jumping, jet-boating or canyon swinging, Queenstown is a thrill-seeker's paradise. The year-round action is supplemented with skiing in winter and water sports in summer.

There is far more to the town than just white-knuckled experiences. On the edge of Lake Wakatipu, with the Remarkables and the Eyre Mountains forming a majestic backdrop, Queenstown is inordinately photogenic. The town itself is fairly compact, meandering up the hills from the lakeside. The Skyline Gondola is a cable car ride to the summit of Bob's Peak, which affords panoramic views of the city below. With much to explore in close proximity to Queenstown, it serves as an ideal base for the region.

isolated landscapes

Glenorchy sits at the northern tip of Lake Wakatipu. Around 40 minutes by car from Queenstown, this small township is surrounded by mountains, glacier-fed rivers and beech forest. It is also home to many tramping tracks, one of them being the Glenorchy end of the Routeburn Track, one of the nine Great Walks in New Zealand. The journey to Glenorchy is magical—the drive passes by Lake Wakatipu, hanging valleys, sheer mountains and a remarkably unspoiled countryside.

THIS PAGE (FROM TOP): A ride on the Shotover Jet in Queenstown is not only a rush to the senses, but also showcases some of the superb landscapes in the area; the Yellow-Eyed Penguin can be found along the rugged southeast coast of the South Island.

OPPOSITE: Skiing opportunities are a major draw to Queenstown. Here, a ski lift is in the process of transporting skiers to the top of the mountains.

...Queenstown is armed with a reputation for being the adventure capital of the world.

rustic charm

Only a 15-minute drive away from Queenstown, Arrowtown is a town steeped in history. In 1862, the discovery of gold in the Arrow River prompted a gold rush and a subsequent settlement of Europeans. It wasn't long before the gold petered out and the miners drifted off elsewhere. Nevertheless a small settlement remained. A pocket of loveliness, Arrowtown is a place steeped in folklore, with leafy villa-lined streets and historic buildings making this a unique location. Aside from sightseeing, there are craft shops, the Lakes District Museum and even a photography gallery. There are also a number of award-winning restaurants, and vineyards nearby. The surrounding region offers numerous picturesque walks and driving routes.

abundant beauty

In an area dominated by Mount Aspiring (the centrepiece of Mount Aspiring National Park) lies Wanaka, a town in the Central Otago region. When translated from Maori, Wanaka means 'renewal of the soul', an apt name for this holiday location, which has both summer and winter seasons and is based around the many outdoor pursuits available.

Located at the southern end of Lake Wanaka, this town has something new to offer each season. Spring brings out an alpine spirit and with it the mountain bikers and anglers; summer is the perfect time to water-ski, boat or swim in Lake Wanaka or Lake Hawea; autumn reveals a kaleidoscope of colours. In winter Wanaka really comes alive, and the vast ski terrain around the town brings tourists flocking to the area. The Cardrona Alpine Resort and Treble Cone Ski Area are both world-class ski resorts and a mecca for snowboarders.

The Mount Aspiring National Park is every outdoor adventurer's dream. Featuring a range of different landforms—hanging valleys, lake basins and over a hundred glaciers of different shapes and sizes—the opportunities are endless for adventure activities such as mountaineering and rock climbing. Day-trips are very common for most visitors, and many end up extending their stay in the park.

THIS PAGE: Amidst the various craft shops of Arrowtown, pottery figurines proudly mark their domain.
OPPOSITE: Arrowtown is particularly spectacular in autumn, when the golden colours of the trees perfectly frame its colonial architecture.

Arrowtown is a place steeped in folkfore, with historic buildings making this a unique location.

southland region

Encompassing Fiordland, the remote city of Invercargill and the forested hills and coastal dunes of the Catlins, Southland is a world unto itself. The landscapes of Fiordland National Park are some of the most dramatic in New Zealand. In a region dominated by forest and water, within the Fiordland are 14 fiords and five major lakes with steep rainforest-covered mountains rising from their sides. Mitre Peak, Milford and Doubtful Sounds are some of the more famous sights in this World Heritage area. The Milford, Routeburn and Kepler tracks are other notable attractions.

OPPOSITE: The distance in-between the towns and cities of the south often involves travelling long-haul, as shown by the figures stated on the road sign.

BELOW: The South Island is a popular destination for snow sport enthusiasts, who flock to the area to enjoy the numerous winter activities, such as skiing.

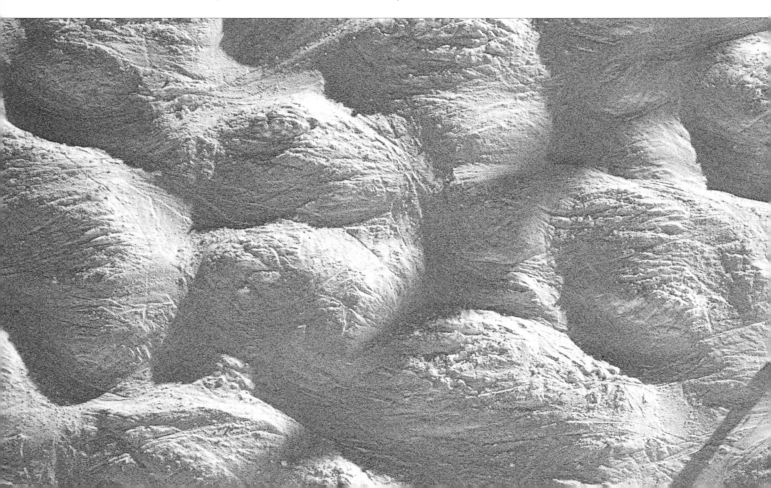

Milford Sound is the most visited of the fiords. Its highlights include the magnificent Mitre Peak and the awe-inspiring Stirling Falls, with sheer rock faces that rise 1,200 m (3,937 ft) or more on either side. Lush rainforests cling precariously onto these cliffs, while seals, penguins, and dolphins frequent the waters. Sometimes misty, sometimes foggy, other times rainy, this area is the epitome of the deepest wilderness. Rudyard Kipling once referred to Milford Sound as the 'eighth wonder of the world'. Though the Fiordland scenery has been described as 'bleak, untouched, ancient and unworldly', there exists a tranquillity here which beguiles the visitor.

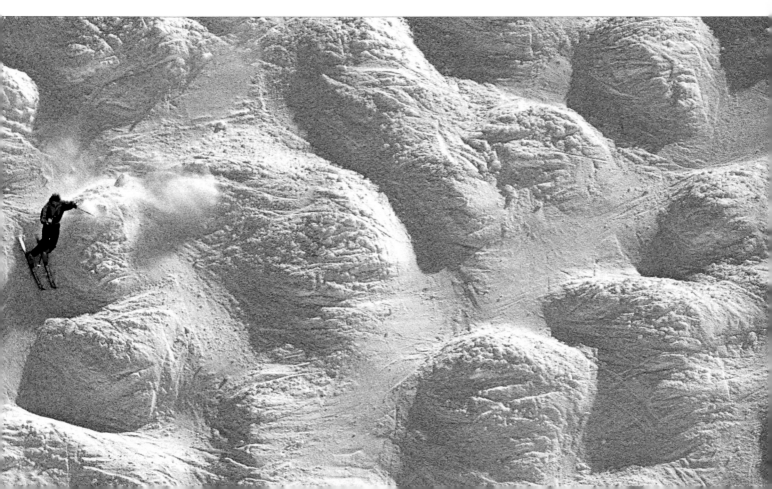

discovering the wonders

There is no other better way to explore the fiords and majestic mountains of Fiordland than by boat. A number of cruises operate in both Milford and Doubtful Sounds, with journeys ranging from a couple of hours to overnight excursions.

The small town of Te Anau is the launch pad to the rest of the region; it is about a two-hour drive to Milford Sound, or a 20-minute journey to Lake Manapouri, the starting point for a Doubtful Sound excursion. Linking Te Anau to Invercargill is the Southern Scenic Route, a tourist highway that passes through native bush, white sandy beaches and colourful coastal fishing villages.

LEFT: *Milford Sound has earned its place as one of the most captivating beauty spots in the world.*
BELOW: *The Hall of Following Faces in Puzzling World, a tourist attraction near Wanaka. In this room, 68 giant models of famous faces 'turn and follow' guests around the room.*

the deep south

Invercargill is New Zealand's southernmost city. It is also the commercial centre of the Southland region. Despite its remote and isolated position, the city exudes unique charm and hospitality. A Scottish settlement from the 1850–60s helped to characterise the city and shape its culture. On display are fine examples of Victorian architecture; also of note are the Southland Museum and Art Gallery. Anderson Park, on the northern boundary of Invercargill, is a large Georgian-style residence that displays the city's extensive collection of New Zealand art. Located 30 km (18.6 miles) southwards is the seaport town of Bluff, and from here visitors can access Stewart Island, an ecological wonderland.

THIS PAGE (FROM TOP): *A tuatara lizard, one of the many diverse species of wildlife to be found on Stewart Island; fishing boats in Halfmoon Bay signify an important way of subsistence in the lives of locals.*

OPPOSITE: *The view from the headland above Mason Bay will leave trampers awestruck.*

PAGE 136: *Sunset over the Moeraki Boulders on the Oekohe Beach, Otago.*

back to nature

Stewart Island is the third-largest island in New Zealand. Sitting demurely in the chilly waters of the Foveaux Strait, Stewart Island lies at the very bottom of the South Island.

This island is a true wilderness retreat in every sense of the word. In 2002, 85 per cent of the Island was converted to become the Rakiura National Park; the 1,746 sq km (674 sq mile) landmass is an unspoilt naturalist's paradise of pristine beaches, rugged coastline and bush-clad hills. It has even been compared to the terrain which the Europeans encountered when they first came to New Zealand.

Called Rakiura ('glowing skies') by the Maori people, the island forms an important part of New Zealand's history. According to legend, when New Zealand was pulled up from the ocean by demigod Maui, Rakiura was the anchor of his canoe.

When Captain Cook first sailed around the area, he couldn't decide whether it was an island or a peninsula; it was only later discovered to be an island by a sealing vessel called the Pegasus, which had set sail from Australia on a sealing expedition. The island was named after the First Officer on that craft, William Stewart, who had been responsible for charting the southern coasts.

Oban, nestling in the picturesque Halfmoon Bay, is the main settlement on this island, and a range of accommodation is available here. The beach is within easy walking distance of the town and there are also some great walking tracks leading through the bush to lookouts or places of historic interest.

The most well-known tramp on Stewart Island is the Rakiura Track, a three-day circuit. It snakes along the coast and through forest areas. The hike is mostly board-walked: this ease of travel coupled with its stunning scenery makes it popular with hikers. There are several other tracks that are less well traversed and perhaps more suitable for the hardy tramper. But whether one comes to enjoy the land or seascapes, a visit to Stewart Island is an experience that will draw the traveller back for more.

...an unspoilt naturalist's paradise of pristine beaches, rugged coastline and bush-clad hills.

blanket bay

...a reflection of New Zealand's colonial architecture.

Picture this: snow-capped mountains lined with dense pine forests and grassy meadows leading towards a sandy beach and turquoise waters. Such is the setting which greets guests upon arrival at Blanket Bay. Located in the Otago district of the South Island, the mountain lodge was built from timber and stone in the traditional style, and sits on the shores of Lake Wakatipu.

With a modern yet classical design, high-beam ceilings and expansive windows framing the views, an atmosphere of elegance resonates throughout the hotel. Polished wood flooring combined with sumptuous fabrics and rugs make rooms a haven for relaxation amidst the rugged outdoors. Each of Blanket Bay's three lodge suites has its own stone fireplace and

THIS PAGE (CLOCKWISE FROM ABOVE):
Lakeside dining is a popular choice with guests at Blanket Bay;
enjoy a leisurely soak in this upscale jacuzzi with a view of the Humboldt mountain range.

OPPOSITE (CLOCKWISE FROM TOP):
The logo of Wyuna Station, one of New Zealand's high country sheep farms;
calming warm hues dominate the lodge's Wine Cave;
high ceilings and wooden beams define this spacious bedroom suite;
summer is an ideal time for a suntan by the heated, outdoor lap pool.

a 37-sq m (400-sq ft) private terrace, which allows one to fully enjoy the lake and mountain views. The lodge's chalets are a reflection of New Zealand's colonial architecture. With the use of schist stone and timber beams, the structure of these chalets complements that of the main lodge.

A day's activities at the lodge tend to be extremely energetic, especially as it offers so many original and exhilarating ways to view and immerse one's self into the scenic haunts surrounding it. Skydive onto the grounds, or take a helicopter ride for a bird's eye view of the local glacier from the front lawn. Hikers also have the exclusive option of experiencing the 'finest walk in the world', to the legendary Milford Sound. Guests can continue to enjoy the outdoors while unwinding at the end of a long day, by having a poolside nap. Back indoors, playing billiards is a 'must' in the Games Room, watched over by the Humboldt mountains. Soak in a steaming jacuzzi, cocktail in hand, while watching the reddish hues of the sunset reflecting off the lake and the snowy peaks beyond.

Blanket Bay's in-house chef, Jason Dell, prepares an à la carte menu which changes daily. His creations ingeniously fuse the exotic flavours of the Pacific Rim with the finest of New Zealand produce. Those with a palate for fine wines can enjoy its offerings of Pinot Noir and Chardonnay—grown and bottled in the Otago region itself—in the intimate ambience of the lodge's Wine Cave.

ROOMS
5 lodge rooms • 3 lodge suites • 4 chalet suites

FOOD
in-house: classical French and contemporary Pacific Rim

DRINK
bar • Wine Room • Wine Cave: New Zealand wines

FEATURES
gym • spa with male and female steam rooms • in-house masseur • helipad • games room • DVD player • heli-skiing • heli-fishing • helicopter tours • hiking • horse riding • jet-boating • bungee jumping • skydiving • rafting

BUSINESS
high-speed Internet access • boardroom

NEARBY
Humboldt mountain range • Wyuna Station • Greenstone river • Caples river • Milford Sound

CONTACT
PO Box 35 Glenorchy, Otago 9350 • telephone: +64.3.441 0115 • facsimile: +64.3.442 9441 • email: information@blanketbay.com • website: www.blanketbay.com

cardrona terrace estate

...a little touch of paradise...

With clear views of bordering mountains and sun-ripened vines meandering to the north, Cardrona Terrace Estate offers the perfect ingredients for a holiday. Located at the base of Cardrona Valley in Central Otago, it is a sanctuary for rest and relaxation in one of the most beautiful locations in New Zealand.

Surrounded by nearly 20 hectares (50 acres) of vineyards and pastures, the property is an ideal platform from which to explore the rugged locale. These vineyards are planted with aromatic white Riesling grapes and Pinot Noir, a delicate variety normally associated with Burgundy in France.

Privacy is assured even though Cardrona Terrace Estate is just 5 minutes from the centre of Wanaka. Run by Sharon and Kevin Alderson, the estate comprises an establishment known as Zingara Lodge, which offers five-star accommodation and fine dining.

Furnished with dramatic Italian lighting and a sleek contemporary design, the interiors are enhanced by the warm tones of handmade tribal rugs and artwork. Sink into a leather chair in the relaxed lounge, calm the senses with soothing music from the vast CD collection or retreat with a favourite book to the lodge's library.

True to the lodge's five-star standards, The Coriander Suite offers an elegant en suite bathroom which features a claw-foot bathtub and an Italian-themed terrazzo vanity and glass basin. The Sage and Thyme Suites have French doors which lead out into the courtyard, overlooking the vineyard. The subtle aroma of organic herbs, olives and nut trees of the

THIS PAGE (CLOCKWISE FROM ABOVE):
The lodge overlooks a serene river; original artwork, tribal rugs and an inviting fireplace liven up this cosy lounge.

OPPOSITE (CLOCKWISE FROM TOP):
Contemporary elements, such as this natural stone sink, dominate throughout the lodge; a yellow-ochre theme adds warmth to the bedroom; modern lighting brightens up the lodge's staircase.

estate's surroundings filters in from the balcony. Here, guests may also enjoy magnificent vistas which extend from Cardrona Valley in the south to Mount Maude in the north, and Black Peak and Mount Avalanche in the west. Every suite is adorned with its own tribal rug, and artwork which provides insights on the country's rich heritage.

Zingara's heated, outdoor spa pool offers a rejuvenating soak amidst the natural surroundings while its tower will be a treat for stargazers. They can access its top floor via a short climb up the ladder, and enjoy an unobstructed view of the sky at night.

The lodge was constructed with eco-friendly factors in mind. A highlight of the building is its use of thermal mass, which traps heat in winter and maximises cool breezes in summer. The materials used for the building itself are carefully chosen to reflect Central Otago's ever-shifting moods and colours.

The awe-inspiring surroundings and interiors of the lodge are matched only by its cuisine. The chef's spécialité du jour changes with the seasons and includes the property's award-winning olive and avocado oil. New Zealand produce features prominently in the menu, especially salmon, which is smoked to perfection, and organically prepared using the lodge's secret recipe. Catch a trout from the nearby lake and the chef will smoke it upon request. Complement a delicately spiced meal with an appropriate wine, such as a high-quality New Zealand Sauvignon Blanc or Pinot Noir. Enjoy it by the roaring fire of the dining room, al fresco on a moonlit deck or in the romantic herb garden.

With Zingara Lodge, the Cardrona Terrace Estate has been described as 'a little touch of paradise', owing to the generous hospitality of its amicable hosts.

ROOMS
5 suites

FOOD
dining room • al fresco or in-suite dining

DRINK
wine cellar

FEATURES
high-speed Internet access • outdoor spa pool • wheelchair-access rooms • pétanque • mountain bikes • archery and target shooting • gym • beauty treatment • aromatherapy

NEARBY
Maude Winery • The Transport Museum • Matukituki Valley • Lake Wanaka • Mount Aspiring • Milford Sound • Wanaka Skydive • fishing • helicopter flights • skiing

CONTACTS
84 Morris Road, RD 2, Wanaka 9382 • telephone: +64.3.443 8020 • facsimile: +64.3.443 1137 • email: info@cardronaterrace.com • website: www.cardronaterrace.com

claremont country estate

...a treasure trove of history and palaeontology.

Spread over 960 hectares (2,400 acres) in Canterbury, near Christchurch, Claremont Country Estate is not only a working sheep, cattle and deer station; it also has its own private nature reserve, and the river close by is a treasure trove of history and palaeontology.

Here, guests are privy to one of the region's most notable and historic country homes. The accommodation at Claremont Country Estate is exclusive and limited to only 10 guests, with five country-style lodge suites. Set on vast park-like grounds and surrounded by rivers and rugged mountain scenery, this is a rare combination of luxury and nature. Guests have a full run of this heritage-listed house, furnished elegantly with fine antiques and lush fabrics. Each suite offers generous views over the gardens and mountains. Handmade tiles, de-mist mirrors with theatrical lighting and claw-foot bathtubs accessorise the en suite bathroom.

Mood lighting and a sophisticated sound system make for unforgettable romantic encounters. Two spacious living rooms with sumptuous sofas and a charming fireplace are great areas in which to kick back and relax.

With an in-house chef creating sublime dishes using the freshest local produce harvested from the lodge's own gardens and orchard, and high-quality meat such as Cervena (certified premier-farmed New Zealand venison) on the menu, mealtimes are equally inspiring at Claremont. Hosted pre-dinner drinks help guests prepare for a convivial evening and work up an appetite for the four-course dinner served communally in the pavilion dining room. Guests who may wish to dine separately are catered for as well.

*THIS PAGE (CLOCKWISE FROM ABOVE):
Accented in white and burgundy, the chequered flooring adds an interesting dimension to the en suite bathroom; the Rose Suite features a Victorian mahogany four-post queen-size bed with a matching dressing table.*

OPPOSITE (FROM TOP): Discover Waipara Gorge, one of Canterbury's abundant geological wonders; an open fireplace warms the cosy lounge, which leads to a garden; Claremont's traditional roof and verandah reveal its country-style influence.

ROOMS
4 deluxe rooms • 1 superior room •
3 three-bedroom cottages

FOOD
in-house chef • pavilion dining room •
conservatory dining room

DRINK
local Waipara wines

FEATURES
private nature reserve • guided
walks and hikes on Claremont private
estate • fishing • horse riding •
river swimming • mountain biking •
tennis • badminton • croquet •
four-wheel drive Land Rover expedition

NEARBY
Nor'wester restaurant • Waipara river •
Waipara wineries • Hanmer Springs
thermal pools • whale watching

CONTACT
828 Ram Paddock Road,
Waipara Gorge, RD 2, Amberley
7482, North Canterbury •
telephone: +64.3.314 7559 •
facsimile: +64.3.314 7065 •
email: relax@claremont-estate.com •
website: www.claremont-estate.com

Outside, vine-clad verandahs, stone-walled courtyards, rose gardens and carefully manicured lawns make a perfect setting for languorous strolls or a peaceful read under one of the numerous mature specimen trees. At the heart of all this natural splendour is a 65-million-year-old boulder fountain which serves as an outstanding centrepiece. It is no wonder that Claremont Country Estate is also a popular wedding and honeymoon venue.

When it comes to itineraries, Claremont features activities and experiences to suit every taste—from exploring the spectacular landscape to the most exciting sporting adventures to be found anywhere. A highlight for guests is an exclusive ride on a guided Land Rover safari tour through its private nature reserve, where a river's twists and turns reveal hidden pre-historic treasures dating back to a time when this land once lay under the sea. It's an adventure so amazing that it has been acclaimed by *Destinations* magazine as 'the most interesting and diverse four-wheel drive experience in NZ'—truly breathtaking!

Though Claremont might seem as though it is greatly distanced from the rest of civilisation, it can be accessed with great ease. Just a 45-minute drive from Christchurch airport, it is an unbeatable base from which to explore Christchurch and Canterbury. Yet for solace seekers, it still serves as a secluded hideaway in which to escape from the world.

eichardt's private hotel

...a kaleidoscope of deep, chocolate browns, rich creams and ochres.

THIS PAGE: *Unwind with a coffee or martini at The House Bar.*

OPPOSITE (CLOCKWISE FROM TOP): *The generously proportioned bathroom includes underfloor heating and adjacent walk-in dressing rooms; possum fur blankets grace this super king-size bed; leaf through a book by the fireplace in complete privacy; The House Bar's layout encourages warm interaction among guests.*

Built during the gold rush in the late 1800s and rescued from demolition in 1999, Eichardt's Private Hotel sits on the waterfront of the stunning Lake Wakatipu in Queenstown, South Island. Steeped in history and providing some of the most breathtaking views of the dramatic Remarkables mountain range, this jewel box of a boutique hotel has set an unbeatable international standard for style, luxury and personalised service.

With its signature white Victorian façade, sash windows and intricate black wrought iron balconies, Eichardt's oozes sophistication from the outside in. Renovated by a leading New Zealand interior designer, the hotel's interiors are characterised by a tasteful mélange of antiques and curios from around the world, counterpoised with sumptuous furnishings in a kaleidoscope of deep, chocolate browns, rich creams and ochres. Sink into an 18th-century English leather armchair by a roaring fire in The Parlour to take breakfast or evening cocktails, amid walls bedecked with original artworks and gold Rococo mirrors. Wood and ivory-marble floors shimmer beneath the earthy tones of velvety rugs to create an atmosphere of contemporary opulence which distinctly reflects Eichardt's identity.

Each of the suites has glorious views over the lake or the mountains, and it is the careful attention to detail which sets them in a league of their own. The possum-fur throw rug on the super king-size bed, heated floors, mirrors in the dark, wood-panelled bathroom, and even a dressing room, feature in every suite. Guests can put their feet up in front of an open fire and sample from a complimentary platter of aged New Zealand cheeses and bottled port: all in the privacy of their own, beautifully

appointed living room. Those with a penchant for exhausting, activity-filled days will certainly relish the creature comforts of the hotel's five spacious suites.

A day of hiking, bungee jumping and jet-boating surely deserves a fitting finale. Wind down at The House Bar with views of Lake Wakatipu, before stepping out into the hustle and bustle of Queenstown's café district where visitors can experience New Zealand's finest cuisine in chic restaurants.

Being a boutique hotel, Eichardt's is able to offer the kind of service that others can only dream of.

A guest's every whim—from a spontaneous request to drift down the valley in a hot air balloon, to a meal served at the hotel by one of Queenstown's gourmet eateries—is accommodated by Eichardt's Private Hotel's staff, for whom nothing seems to be too much of a hassle.

ROOMS
5 suites

FOOD
The Parlour: breakfast •
The House Bar: lunch

DRINK
The House Bar: local wines and cocktails

FEATURES
integrated entertainment systems • mini-bar • in-suite massages • spa

BUSINESS
high-speed Internet access

NEARBY
Lake Wakatipu • hiking in national parklands • skydiving • jet-boating • white water rafting • heli-skiing • bungee jumping • mountain biking • fishing • wineries • shopping • dining

CONTACT
Marine Parade, Queenstown 9348 • telephone: +64.3.441 0450 • facsimile: +64.3.441 0440 • email: stay@eichardtshotel.co.nz • website: www.eichardts.co.nz

hapuku lodge

...carefully selected to reflect the colours and textures of Kaikoura's landscape.

THIS PAGE (FROM ABOVE): A pathway leads to the back of the eco-friendly Hapuku Lodge; the Kaikoura Seaward mountain range is a fitting backdrop for Hapuku's Tree Houses.
OPPOSITE (CLOCKWISE FROM TOP): The Tree House bedroom interior is inspired by country living, but with a modern touch; two-toned vases contrast with a Hapuku River stone fireplace; lounge in the spacious, earth-toned living room of the Olive House Apartment.

On the northeastern coast of the South Island lies the picturesque town of Kaikoura. Known as a 'virtual marine Serengeti', a term coined by *NZ Geographic*, it is an ecological paradise, where swimming with dolphins and seals in the sea and watching whales dive towards the ocean depths are everyday events. Here is where Hapuku Lodge sits, nestled between the Kaikoura Seaward mountain range and Mangamaunu Bay, on a deer and olive farm.

Owned and designed by the Wilson family, the lodge was created as a contemporary country inn with the aim of providing 'a great night's sleep in one of the most beautiful places in the world.' One of the striking features of the lodge is the luxurious Tree House accommodation. Brightly coloured, each room is fitted with custom-designed and locally handcrafted furniture. A sunroom with heated tile floors, ipod with Bose sound system, wide-screen TV, large spa bath, air conditioning, and, as with the rest of the guestrooms, Hapuku Lodge's custom-made beds and mattresses, are generously put in place to ensure utmost comfort and relaxation for weary travellers. Views over immaculate olive groves and deer paddocks complement one's bath. Two of the Tree Houses also include a second-level bedroom, en suite, and twin decks, ideal for families or small groups travelling together.

These Tree Houses are designed to be a modern complement to the native environment. Natural materials were carefully selected to reflect the colours and textures of Kaikoura's landscape. Native woods and green-tinged copper clad the exteriors, while large windows and earthen tones bring the tree canopy from outside to in. Affording the most breathtaking views on the property, the Tree Houses are well-placed amid the branches of Manuka Grove.

In a lodge where every detail has been fully considered and every need anticipated, one can expect the dining experience to be nothing less than impressive. A stylish and contemporary dining room, Hapuku Café was cleverly re-designed by the lodge owners and designers Tony and Peter Wilson into Hapuku Dining Room and Lounge, to accommodate larger groups of diners.

Guests are offered a three-course dinner, with venison and Kaikoura's famed crayfish as specialities, and a continental breakfast buffet. The large dining room can also be used to host events for up to 60 people. A central stone fireplace splits the space to provide a private and intimate area for meetings or small gatherings. Doubtless, the comments around the dinner table will ring with compliments for this blissful rural retreat.

ROOMS
1 Olive House Apartment •
3 King Rooms • 3 Queen Rooms •
5 one-bedroom Tree Houses •
2 Family Tree Houses

FOOD
Hapuku Dining Room and Lounge: continental breakfast buffet and local dinner • common or private dining

DRINK
New Zealand wine list

FEATURES
iPod stereo system • in-house movie selection • heated towel rails and bathroom floors • spa bath • catering services

BUSINESS
conference facilities • wireless high-speed Internet access

NEARBY
Kaikoura city centre • sea-kayaking • deep-sea fishing • whale watching • swimming with dolphins and seals • Maori cultural tours • mountain biking • hiking • surfing

CONTACT
State Highway 1, Station Road, RD 1, Kaikoura 7371 •
telephone: +64.3.319 6559 •
facsimile: +64.3.319 6557 •
email: info@hapukulodge.com •
website: www.hapukulodge.com

hotel off the square

...'new age modernism with a hint of Pacific fusion'.

When a hotel is owned and managed by a designer, aesthetic innovation and cultural stimulation are only to be expected. Hotel Off The Square surpasses such expectations and is a highly individual and original bohemian-chic boutique hotel, with surprises tucked into every niche. Although the hotel is part of the Accor group, its design, ethos and control remain firmly within the grip of designer and owner Timothy Nicholls.

This cutting-edge art house is known for its superb location and serves as an ideal base from which to enjoy the delights of Christchurch, the lively city on New Zealand's South Island. With the city tram running quietly through it, this is convenience and historic revivalism at its best.

Hotel Off The Square is located right by the central city square and is mere metres from Christchurch's prime attractions such as fashionable shopping malls and Cathedral Square. It is truly a Kiwi-inspired lifestyle project situated close to trendy restaurants and bars at The Strip, and is part of the Cathedral Junction glass atrium.

The hotel itself is geographically, metaphorically and literally, 'off the square'. A new development styled on New York boutique hotels, its 38 rooms are geometrically unpredictable. Be it for particularly tall guests, independent women travelling alone, business

THIS PAGE (FROM ABOVE): Expect to meet eye-catching and thought-provoking artwork interspersed throughout the hotel's interior; the city tram welcomes passengers right from the hotel's reception area.

OPPOSITE (CLOCKWISE FROM TOP): Paintings by New Zealand's creative artists are proudly displayed on the corridor walls; the colour scheme fittingly reflects the sights of Central Otago and Canterbury; warm, bright hues decorate the bedroom, which embraces Manhattan-style urban living.

ROOMS
38 rooms

FOOD
Seasons: breakfast and lunch café •
Bi Bi's: fusion of Chinese and Japanese •
Maitea Maison: Spanish •
Bluefish: Japanese

DRINK
a range of mostly New Zealand wines

FEATURES
city tram service at doorstep •
satellite TV • New Zealand artwork

BUSINESS
high-speed Internet access •
Ethernet access • secretarial and
courier services

NEARBY
Cathedral Square • The Strip: bars
and restaurants • Botanical Gardens •
fashion shopping • museum •
art galleries

CONTACT
115 Worcester Street, Christchurch
0800 • telephone: +64.3.374 9980 •
facsimile: +64.3.374 9987 •
email: enquiries@offthesquare.co.nz •
website: www.offthesquare.co.nz

executives, or those with a keen eye for cutting-edge design, colour and materials, there is a great variety of rooms. Each features a unique theme, allowing the hotel's amiable staff to place guests in a room which best suits their needs. Designer Timothy describes the overall concept as 'new age modernism with a hint of Pacific fusion'.

The stylish accommodation ranges from studio chic and deluxe level rooms to family or adventure rooms. To showcase local talent and indigenous materials, Hotel Off The Square uses 100 per cent pure New Zealand wool blankets in slate grey, dovetailing the colour palette of the hotel with its local urban environment. The Danish-inspired window drapes use rich McQuarrie wool to ensure full blackout and a deep, uninterrupted sleep. The furniture is covered in a new 'slick and sleek' textile fabric, accentuating the hotel's designer features.

Hotel Off The Square is an all-in-one getaway for leisure, business and cultural travellers in the heart of the city. It has elegance and simplicity alongside striking interiors and individual pieces of art. Design and functionality co-exist to create a cosy, private-club feel—the complete antithesis of the homogenised hotels so prevalent today. Evocative Paul Jackson artwork, New Zealand pop art and contemporary photography ensure that memories of their unique stay will be firmly etched in the minds of guests long after their urban New Zealand visit has ended.

huntley house

...his love for plants is evident in the verdant greenery surrounding the property.

Huntley House was originally built in 1876 by one of Christchurch's early settlers, J.H. Twentyman. In 1971, the property was bought by its current owners, the Reid family, who transformed it into a world-class boutique hotel in 2004. The style of hospitality here is warm and traditional, and the experience is akin to staying with family friends in a colonial home.

Located in a private setting among lawns and gardens, it is easy to forget that Huntley House is situated just minutes from Christchurch airport and the city centre. Its original owner, Twentyman, was the president of the Horticultural Society. His love for plants is evident in the verdant greenery surrounding the property. Stroll through the grounds and marvel at the countless shrubs, flowers and trees that have been lovingly planted and nurtured for over a century. Huntley House is a wonderful place to spend the afternoon by relaxing in its serenity.

The house offers 17 bedrooms located in the Homestead Rooms, Garden Rooms, Garden Suites and Apartments. Traditionally furnished, they all feature king- or super king-size beds, with all the modern conveniences expected of a luxury hotel. For instance, each en suite bathroom has a spa bath and separate shower with either a massage head or monsoon head.

THIS PAGE (CLOCKWISE FROM ABOVE): Engage in a challenging game of chess at the library; relax indoors or closer to nature on the balcony in the Garden Room.

OPPOSITE (FROM TOP): Indulge in an enticing lunch with speciality wines; dining at Huntley House is an elegant yet tranquil experience; lush greenery surrounds the two-storey house.

ROOMS
4 Homestead Rooms •
4 Garden Rooms • 4 Garden Suites •
2 two-bedroom Apartments

FOOD
in-house chef • dining room

DRINK
bar • mini-bars in rooms

FEATURES
library • billiards room • heated
outdoor pool • tennis • golf

NEARBY
Aoraki Balloon Safaris • Brighton Pier •
Christchurch Casino • Christchurch
Tramway • Harewood Golf Club •
Terrace Downs Golf Resort • swimming
with dolphins • whale watching

CONTACT
67 Yaldhurst Road, Upper Riccarton,
Christchurch 8042 •
telephone: +64.3.348 8435 •
facsimile: +64.3.341 6833 •
email: reservations@huntleyhouse.co.nz •
website: www.huntleyhouse.co.nz

The Garden Suites feature a separate living area, with an oversized couch, cosy fireplace and a full home entertainment system. Well-equipped kitchens, with dining tables and living areas in the Apartments make them ideal for longer-term or family visits. More intimate settings can be found in the Garden Rooms, which provide luxurious amenities, gas log fireplaces, plus verandahs which offer calming views of the heated pool and sprawling gardens beyond.

Dining at Huntley House is an experience in itself. In the breakfast room, homestead-style breakfasts are served piping hot from the kitchen, while in the afternoon, high tea is served on fine china in either the bar, library or formal dining room. Lunch and dinner are renowned, as Huntley House's chef creates an inviting menu using seasonal ingredients which showcase the freshness and essence of Canterbury cuisine. The accompanying wine list has been carefully selected to represent the best of Old and New World wines.

Canterbury is famous for its natural beauty, and guests need not travel far to experience a wide range of activities and adventure. The region's tourism opportunities include taking to the skies in a hot air balloon, basking in natural hot pools, visiting one of New Zealand's leading arts venues, taking a stroll along the pier at New Brighton Beach, touring the inner city of Christchurch on a historic tram or playing on one of the country's top golf courses—the possibilities are endless.

kincaid lodge

...from stylish escapism to adrenalin-fuelled adventure.

Kincaid Lodge is, both metaphorically and geographically, at the height of South Island. Located high up on the east coast, 6 km (4 miles) north of Kaikoura, this exclusive boutique accommodation boasts everything from stylish escapism to adrenalin-fuelled adventure—complementary Kiwi extremes!

With a century-spanning history, this homestead still operates a small cattle farm—a vestige of its hardworking past. Its breathtaking surroundings have changed little in this time, with the shimmering blue of the Pacific in the distance and the glints thrown by the snow-capped mountains still interrupting the far-off horizon.

Owned and managed by New Zealander Helen Costley and Barry Chandler, Kincaid Lodge is the epitome of Antipodean luxury at its best. The three spacious guest rooms are exquisitely appointed, each inspired by Helen's discerning taste and inherent eye for style. All of them feature sumptuous en suites and have private verandahs that open out into the large gardens, with dramatic mountain and sea views forming the backdrop on all sides. Complete with polished wood, gleaming charcoal tiles and high-quality fittings, the bathrooms pre-empt every request, coming fully equipped with high-end beauty products and bathrobes.

The entire lodge is individually decorated and exudes the warming, personal feel of a unique 'home away from home', with indulgent touches like freshly baked cookies and handmade chocolates savoured by a roaring log-fire.

THIS PAGE (FROM BELOW): **Nestled at the foot of majestic snow-capped mountains, a redefining experience at the lodge, with its spacious surrounds, awaits; every room comes complete with an en suite and offers a breathtaking view of the sunset right at the doorstep.**

OPPOSITE (FROM TOP): **A private corner provides the perfect setting for guests to unwind; the bedroom décor tickles one's fancy with its comfort in pure luxury and tranquillity.**

ROOMS
2 queen rooms • 1 super king or twin room

FOOD
Continental and home-cooked breakfast

FEATURES
mountain and sea views • complementary wireless hotspot • private patio • electric blankets • homemade cookies and chocolates • lounge with piano and guitar • CD player • TV and games • friendly sheep dogs to walk • whale watching • cultural tours • mountain biking • golf • tennis • pétanque • croquet

NEARBY
Christchurch International Airport • Mount Lyford ski field • Hanmer Springs thermal resort • helipad on site

CONTACTS
611 Main North Road, RD 1, Kaikoura 7371 • telephone: +64.3.319 6851 • facsimile: +64.3.319 6801 • email: helen@kincaidlodge.co.nz • website: www.kincaidlodge.co.nz

Equally impressive is the exterior of the lodge. The perfectly manicured gardens are designed to encourage the light-hearted playing of pétanque, badminton or tennis. Further afield, opportunities abound for golf, sea or fly-fishing and rigorous bushwalks. Highly acclaimed wineries of the Marlborough region are also found to be within close proximity.

The Kaikoura Peninsula truly is an unparalleled region for getting closer to nature. Its stunning scenery is amply dappled with beautiful flora and fauna, and seal colonies. One of the world's most exciting areas for ocean birds, the region also possesses the greatest variety of birds in New Zealand.

Adventure seekers will appreciate the vast array of activities in the area—Maori, nocturnal or wilderness walks, quad biking and swimming with dolphins. The lodge even enjoyed the spotlight of celebrity with the presence of Diarmuid Gavin and the film crew of *No Frontiers*, and more recently, when the team behind the Australian hit show, *The Great Outdoors*, sojourned there whilst capturing whale watching footage nearby.

The pinnacle of any visit should be a session with talented therapist Belinda from the nearby Body and Soul Spa. From the rejuvenation of an 'Ultimate Escape' package to a pre-wedding 'Bride To Be' session, this experience is guaranteed to ease the soul, clear the mind and prepare the body for another brilliant day at Kincaid Lodge.

the lodge at paratiho farms

...one of just three luxurious Relais & Chateaux properties in New Zealand.

One of just three Relais & Chateaux properties in New Zealand, The Lodge at Paratiho Farms, nestled in 809 hectares (2,000 acres) of pristine and secluded working farmland, is described as one of the finest and most luxurious accommodations in the country.

Lavishly decorated in a refreshing blend of classic and modern styles, the main building at Paratiho (Maori for 'paradise') consists of a palatial house that is filled with New Zealand and international artwork and sculptures, adding flashes of colour and wit.

Separate from the main lodge are six spacious suites, each positioned within the 8-hectare (20-acre) grounds for utmost exclusivity. Every suite provides a large walk-in wardrobe, laptop with high-speed Internet access, fireplace, and for added privacy, a separate bedroom from the lounge area. Each en suite bathroom, complemented by a rainforest shower and claw-foot bathtub, opens onto a private garden of native flora. The suite's underfloor heating extends out onto an outdoor patio area—perfect for stargazers to enjoy viewing the night sky.

The lodge's manicured grounds are looked after by its four gardeners. Lawns lead down to tranquil lakes surrounded by native bush. Inviting pathways bursting with colour take guests on a journey to the swimming pool, scented gardens, and citrus and olive groves. Around the suites, colour gives way to a peaceful white, made up of the 500 rose bushes surrounding the lodge. Neat box hedging borders the croquet green, overlooking the golf course.

Along the way, one is likely to find the Head Chef selecting fresh ingredients in the kitchen garden. Truly a gourmet destination, Paratiho enhances what the Nelson region already has. Tuck into breakfast and lunch at the lodge, or a picnic lunch planned according to guests'

THIS PAGE (CLOCKWISE FROM TOP): **Local and international artwork form an intrinsic feature of the colourful living room; large sheepskin rugs surround the opulent four-post bed; indulge in a warm bath that is refreshingly close to nature.**

OPPOSITE (CLOCKWISE FROM TOP): **Come evening, the lodge lights up to create a splendid reflection on a calm river surface; the front lawn is filled with a myriad of quirky sculptures; a display of dynamic artwork complements a feast for eight; pick up a culinary tip or two at the Paratiho Cooking School.**

preferences. Savour the lodge's five-course dinner, prepared in an open-concept kitchen. A wide range of beverages is offered. This includes wines, champagne, cocktails and spirits. A mini-bar is also available in each suite.

In keeping with its aim to pamper guests in style, the lodge's Health and Beauty Spa, a winner of 'New Zealand's Leading Spa' of the World Travel Awards in 2004 and 2005, awaits. With treatments ranging from facials, manicures and hair styling to massage, hydrotherapy treatments and body wraps, the spa is designed to soothe the mind and body.

Take advantage of the lodge's activities such as swimming, tennis, golf, pétanque and croquet, or work out at the well-equipped gym, complete with a saunarium (steam and sauna room). Alternatively, enjoy a guided walk or four-wheel drive tours of the property and farm.

Beyond the farm gates are the fruits of the Nelson region. Not only does the area supply flavoursome and plentiful produce. It also hosts acclaimed artists, three National Parks and some of New Zealand's finest boutique wineries. A 45-minute drive from Nelson Airport is all it takes to reach The Lodge at Paratiho Farms.

ROOMS
6 suites • 1 cottage

FOOD
dining room • al fresco • in-suite dining

DRINK
wine cellar: New Zealand wines

FEATURES
gym • sauna • steam room • outdoor heated infinity-edge pool • golf • pétanque • tennis • croquet • spa and beauty treatments • Paratiho Cooking School

NEARBY
Abel Tasman National Park • Nelson Lakes National Park • Kahurangi National Park • vineyards

CONTACT
545 Waiwhero Road, RD 2, Upper Moutere, Nelson 7175 • telephone: +64.3.528 2100 • facsimile: +64.3.528 2101 • email: lodge@paratiho.co.nz • website: www.paratiho.co.nz

matakauri lodge

...an alpine lakeside retreat.

THIS PAGE: The lounge area is an ideal spot for book lovers to be fully immersed in their favourite pastime. It also allows guests to enjoy awe-inspiring views of the lakes and mountains from the comfort of the lodge.

OPPOSITE (FROM TOP): A short stroll through the native bush surroundings leads one to the villas; the lodge offers a splendid juxtaposition of the mountain range and cobalt-blue sky; guests can feel the cool breeze from the lake flowing through without leaving the bathtub.

Queenstown is renowned for being a haven to adventure seekers. Yet at the same time, it is also increasingly luring discerning guests in search of tranquillity and breathtaking mountain scenery. Just minutes away from this town is Matakauri Lodge, an exclusive retreat perched on the edge of Lake Wakatipu.

The lodge offers two types of accommodation. The four villas—each spanning 63 sq m (700 sq ft)—come replete with space and privacy. The capacious bathrooms feature twin vanities, double showers and two-person spa baths. A separate lounge allows guests to laze comfortably in the window seat or by the log fire. The lounge also has an outdoor terrace—perfect for soaking in the panoramic views of the pristine lake and snow-capped mountains.

Based in the main lodge building are the three stylishly executed suites. The king-size beds are draped in the finest linen and the bathrooms feature large showers or deep tubs, depending on which suite one selects. Wakatipu Suite, for instance, is uniquely angled to welcome maximum sunlight throughout the day while Matakauri Suite has unobstructed views of the majestic Remarkables mountain range to Walter Peak.

ROOMS
4 villas • 3 suites

FOOD
private or outdoor dining

DRINK
wine cellar

FEATURES
satellite TV • fireplace • two-person bath • Direct Dial telephone • CD player • gym • library • sauna • massage • outdoor hot tub

NEARBY
'*Lord of the Rings*' tour by road or air • Queenstown Golf Club • Milford Sound • winery tours • glacier tours • guided hikes • horse riding

CONTACTS
Glenorchy Road, PO Box 888, Queenstown 7467 • telephone: +64.3.441 1008 • facsimile: +64.3.441 2180 • email: relax@matakauri.co.nz • website: www.matakauri.co.nz

When winter arrives, the underfloor heating, roaring fireplace, heated towel rails and pure wool blankets keep the shivers at bay. In summer, cooling breezes waft through the vast windows while chilled wine awaits in the minibar in each suite. Needless to say, comfort at the lodge is a priority whatever the season may be.

Diversions abound with a well-stocked library and innumerable bush or lakeside walking routes, accompanied by the hypnotic lapping of the lake. With such a quaint and picturesque alpine environment, work-related worries are bound to dissipate into the fresh mountain air.

Self-indulgence is made possible with the luxury of two massage therapy rooms, a sauna and outdoor hot tub. Alternatively, guests may want to request for an aromatherapy bath in their room. Specialising in a range of holistic treatments, the in-house massage therapists use only natural and organic products made on the premises itself.

Matakauri Lodge excels in the provision of exquisitely fresh cuisine and award-winning local wine in intimate settings. Dine in the atmospheric cellar itself, on a private balcony beneath a vibrant sunset or next to the inviting fireplace in the elegant dining room. The impeccably presented entrées include quail, soba noodle and spinach entrée, with golden pork loin and asparagus as a principal dish. Other signatures include luscious desserts such as iced milk chocolate and butterscotch terrine or simply, hearty breakfasts.

Every conceivable activity is available in the vicinity, from Pinot Noir tastings at top Otago wineries to extreme skiing in the Remarkables at Coronet Peak. As a self-sufficient destination or a base from which to explore this phenomenal corner of the world, Matakauri Lodge offers an alpine lakeside retreat.

millbrook

...designed by master golfer Sir Bob Charles.

THIS PAGE (CLOCKWISE FROM ABOVE):
Millbrook is set against the Remarkables mountain range; minimalism prevails throughout the luxurious Fairway Home; this Villa bedroom is both warm and welcoming.

OPPOSITE (CLOCKWISE FROM TOP):
Therapeutic scented candles; abundant lavender surrounds the Village Inn exterior; the cottage lounge embraces a country theme; flowers setting the mood for a relaxing spa treatment.

A unique getaway is not the only thing on the Millbrook agenda—discerning travellers can count 'warm' and 'welcoming' in as well. Location-wise, it is close enough to reach the cosmopolitan buzz of Queenstown, but far enough into the alpine countryside for a taste of seclusion and tranquillity.

All accommodation options are beautifully appointed. Village Inns come with entertainment systems, essential for movie buffs, while the larger suites have a fireplace and a dining table or kitchenette. The rooms are finished with a light, French provincial touch and each has a private patio with views over the omnipresent mountains and perfectly maintained Millbrook grounds. The spacious bathrooms feature deep tubs and luxuriant bathrobes.

Millbrook's expansive premises include an 18-hole championship golf course, indoor and outdoor pools, two spas, a sauna, and one of the country's top facilities, The Spa at Millbrook. Indulge in its assortment of beauty, massage and purifying treatments.

The 18-hole par 72 course was designed by master golfer Sir Bob Charles. Set in a natural, alpine amphitheatre with the Remarkables mountain range as a backdrop, Millbrook's course showcases New Zealand golf at its best. Fittingly, Millbrook's premium accommodation option is Fairway Home, which ensures the walk to the first hole is kept to a minimum distance.

Golf widows will be spoilt for choice too. The tennis courts or fully equipped health and fitness centre are just the place to set pulses racing. Alternatively, sign up for one of the plethora of activities available in the nearby adventure hub of Queenstown.

Lovers of fine food have four individual venues to choose from. The Clubhouse, which overlooks the undulating golf course, has an innovative menu that fuses classic European influences with contemporary culinary twists from New Zealand. Dine al fresco with a view of the 18th hole, or savour a brandy by its roaring log fire. Trace the aroma of freshly ground coffee to The Millhouse where chefs cater to guests' fancies in an open kitchen, cooking up a storm with local ingredients of the highest quality. Fine local wines such as Central Otago Pinot Gris, available at The Hole-in-One Bar, seem to taste better when accompanied by the balmy, midsummer mountain air. Fans of Japanese cuisine will quickly become enamoured with the fusion of traditional and modern flavours at Sala Sala.

With a dedicated and intuitive team, Millbrook has been the venue of choice for major companies, such as New Zealand Asset Management Ltd. Whether for golf, business or leisure, this is indeed the ultimate Queenstown address.

ROOMS
51 Village Inns • 70 Village Suites • 13 Hotel Villas • 40 Cottages • 8 Fairway Homes

FOOD
The Clubhouse: brasserie-style • The Millhouse: European • Sala Sala Restaurant: Japanese

DRINK
The Hole-in-One Bar

FEATURES
private patios • mini-bar • 18-hole championship golf course • driving range • The Spa at Millbrook • health and fitness centre

BUSINESS
conference facilities • high-speed Internet access

NEARBY
historic Arrowtown

CONTACT
Malaghans Road, Arrowtown, Queenstown 9371 • telephone: +64.3.441 7000 • facsimile: +64.3.441 7007 • email: reservations@millbrook.co.nz • website: www.millbrook.co.nz

sherwood lodge

...the ideal setting for rest and relaxation.

THIS PAGE (CLOCKWISE FROM ABOVE):
*Enjoy a nap outdoors in
a hammock against a
mountainous backdrop;
an architectural masterpiece
greets guests upon arrival;
The Burbury Suite enjoys
generous sunlight.*

OPPOSITE (FROM TOP): *Horse treks
bring guests across rivers
and mountain passes;
table d'hôte dining is
an elegant affair;
The White Room comes
with a luxurious super
king-size bed.*

Given today's fast-paced world, many travellers search for places with a slower and more laid-back vibe when it comes to holidays. It is exactly for such travellers that the idea to run Sherwood Lodge as a luxury destination was conceived. Situated north of Christchurch in a remote river valley at the foot of two mountain ranges, Sherwood Lodge offers a taste of the carefree life. Here, there are no noisy distractions, crowds or deadlines to meet. Instead, forgotten pleasures such as big skies and wide-open spaces, lively conversations enjoyed in deep armchairs in front of open fires, and warm hospitality for small, intimate groups abound.

Originally built in 1910 as a farmer's homestead, the lodge was purchased by its current owners, Craig Aitken and Phillipa Turley, in 2000. Using their experiences as both tourists and business travellers, they personally supervised the transformation of the property into the warm and welcoming home that it is today.

Nothing was overlooked in the quest to create the ideal setting for rest and relaxation. Three junior suites and two standard rooms have each been skilfully crafted to provide a cosy ambience for guests to unwind in, with fresh flowers, bathrobes and fruit bowls greeting them on arrival. The 50-sq m (565-sq ft) Burbury Suite, which was once the library and manager's office, will win the hearts of guests with its romantically-draped bedroom and direct access to a private lounge.

A similar attention to detail has gone into the dining experience. Meals with a distinct North Canterbury flavour are served either in the communal dining room with a four-course table d'hôte menu or in an intimate setting for two in the room. Summer, in particular, is an

ROOMS
3 junior suites • 2 standard rooms

FOOD
common or in-suite dining

DRINK
wine cellar

FEATURES
outdoor pool • spa pool • horse trekking • tennis • pétanque • river walks • fossil hunts • farm tours • mountain bikes • picnics • library

NEARBY
Amuri Mountains • Hanmer Springs • Mount Lyford • Waiau River • Waipara wineries • skiing • jet-boat rides • four-wheel drives • whale and dolphin watching • fishing • Maori tours • hunting • farm tours • hiking • golf • art and craft tours • massage

CONTACTS
919 Sherwood Road, RD 1, Waiau, North Canterbury 8275 • telephone: +64.3.315 6078 • facsimile: +64.3.315 6424 • email: sherwoodlodge@xtra.co.nz • website: www.sherwoodlodge.co.nz

opportune time to relish a hearty breakfast on the balcony, which offers spectacular mountain views. When evening arrives, a casual dining experience beneath a breathtaking 2-m (7-ft) high glass dome is also enjoyed during this season. All of the ingredients are derived locally, with a strong emphasis on regional specialities such as Canterbury lamb, venison, crayfish and also salmon from the nearby rivers. The wine list features many of the country's finest vineyards. For a complete culinary experience, the resident butler will be on hand to recommend the most suitable wine to accompany each dish.

Nature has blessed the region with numerous options for outdoor pursuits. These include horse trekking, fair chase hunting in the mountains, fresh and saltwater fishing in the surrounding rivers, bird watching, or simply, lazing in a hammock while taking in the picturesque views. Savouring the peace and serenity at Sherwood Lodge is surely a luxury in itself.

the spire queenstown

...a temple of contemporary design...

THIS PAGE (CLOCKWISE FROM RIGHT):
Sculptures and coffee-table books fill The Spire's lobby; technology meets comfort in each of The Spire rooms; head to the Inspire Bar for a night of food and live music.

OPPOSITE (CLOCKWISE FROM TOP): *Soak in a warm bath while watching a movie with great ease; The Spire Chamber is both a boardroom and dining room; bold colours add visual interest to The Spire bedroom.*

The Spire Queenstown opened its doors in May 2005 when its owners and the General Manager, Mel Bohse, decided that they had finally gotten everything right. The wait was certainly worth it. The Spire Queenstown is a temple of contemporary design, and the only Kiwi property to make it to the 'Hot List' of both the UK and US editions of *Condé Nast Traveler*.

Hidden away on Church Lane, one of the many charming alleys and lanes in lakefront Queenstown, this design shrine boasts plenty of personality wrapped in an ambience of sophistication and impeccable taste. The hotel's 10 restful rooms are tastefully furnished without being ostentatious, featuring monochromatic walls which act as a canvas for New Zealand's talented artists, and designer furniture in rich leather. Each room has a Tiramu basalt fireplace, a large covered balcony and houses design icons of the 21st century—Charles Eames chairs, Philippe Starck lamps, Dedon furniture and Bang & Olufsen phones. For indoor entertainment, guests may feast their eyes on the plasma TV with integrated Windows Media. Above the bathtub are sleek shutter doors which pull back so that guests can unwind and enjoy their favourite movie on DVD while savouring a glass of sparkling champagne.

Little surprises are also left on guests' pillows each night. They include Evolu skincare products which are completely natural and exclusively made in New Zealand. This is almost a necessity for guests who have engaged in a night of fun at the hotel's Inspire Bar.

Based on the concept of an intimate Manhattan-style Jazz bar, the Inspire Bar is the ideal spot for guests to have a chat while enjoying live music by talented artists and sipping delectable cocktails or fine wines. On Friday evenings, performances by popular local jazz

maestros such as Hine Marchand, Brent Muir and Trevor Coleman make for a delightful musical treat. Groove to the tunes of jazz, rhythm-and-blues and Latino music, and watch the cast of stylish guests as they turn up to see and be seen.

Inspire Restaurant's award-winning cuisine offers a culinary journey through fresh local produce, and is highly recommended. The establishment can seat up to 40 for à la carte dining or 30 guests for a private function. Choose from the ten-course Signature Dégustation menu or three- and five-course à la carte menus which are prepared by one of New Zealand's top chefs, Rex Morgan. His creations are an absolute tour de force of delicate and intricate flavours matched perfectly with New Zealand's regional wines.

Do it all again the next morning at breakfast—or more likely, brunch. Begin with a dish of Prosciutto di Parma, Buffalo Mozzarella, Cherry Tomatoes with Avocado Oil and Vincotto. A sweet finale to this meal would be the Vanilla Rice Pudding with Saffron-Poached Pear.

Naturally, in a place as beautiful as Queenstown, guests will want to explore nearby destinations such as Lake Wakatipu. To that end, The Spire's team are armed with a wealth of knowledge of the area and can arrange for activities such as steamboat rides across the lake; flights or cruises to Milford Sound; a private picnic on a mountain top or overlooking a glacier lake, which is accessible only via helicopter; mountain biking down Coronet Peak; jet-boating through Shotover Canyon; or paddling up the Dart River in a Funyak. In addition, a bustling nightlife scene, popular restaurants, bars and shops are recommended to ensure a fruitful holiday for discerning travellers staying at The Spire Queenstown.

ROOMS
10 rooms

FOOD
Inspire Restaurant: contemporary New Zealand

DRINK
Inspire Bar: extensive list of wines, cocktails and spirits

FEATURES
interactive multimedia system • pillow menu • tour desk • complimentary airport transfers • complimentary Wi-Fi • iPod docking stations in all rooms • childcare service

BUSINESS
The Spire Chamber (executive boardroom) • high-speed Internet access • secretarial service

NEARBY
Lake Wakatipu • Southern Alps • Coronet Peak • Shotover Canyon • restaurants • bars • shops • Maori cultural performances • horse riding • hiking • fly-fishing

CONTACT
3–5 Church Lane, PO Box 1129, Queenstown 9300 • telephone: +64.3.441 0004 • facsimile: +64.3.441 0003 • email: queenstown@thespirehotels.com • website: www.thespirehotels.com

takaro

...one of the most untouched landscapes in the world.

THIS PAGE: The resort's glass spa offers a variety of rejuvenating treatments and facilities, all under one roof.

OPPOSITE (CLOCKWISE FROM TOP): Sunset at Takaro is a breathtaking sight; shades of lilac dominate the bedroom in the Water Chalet; the Earth Chalet's living room is decorated with earth tones such as mud chocolate and terracotta.

Located at the lower-end, deep-mountain interior of South Island, Takaro is a long way off the beaten track. Those embarking on this trip for the first time might be forgiven for wondering if they have chosen the right place for their holiday. Fret not, for Takaro's seclusion is just one of the many reasons why making the journey to this destination is even more worthwhile.

Set on a 1,052-hectare (2,600-acre) private estate on the edge of the pristine wilderness that is Fiordland National Park, the property is surrounded by abundant World Heritage forests which form one of the most untouched landscapes in the world. Fittingly, scenes from the movie trilogy *The Lord of the Rings* were filmed in the surrounding grounds.

Accommodation at Takaro is as unique as it is indulgent. Revolving around the themes of wood, fire, earth, metal and water, each of the 10 grass-roofed chalets blends the philosophies of the Chinese five elements, feng shui and *I Ching*. The modern and minimalist design characteristics create an atmosphere of peace and well-being, individually suited to each and every guest. Traditional rooms are also available and stunning views of Upukerora River Valley are standard, as are luxury fixtures such as a spa bath and home theatre system, complete with surround sound. In addition, high-speed Internet access is offered in every room.

Takaro has its own organic farm and gardens, ensuring the kitchen maintains high standards of freshness and quality at all times. Selected ingredients are prepared using a fusion of Western and Chinese influences to create dishes which are original and tangy in flavour. This is gourmet dining at its very finest, and a five-course evening meal here more than justifies the long journey to this remote wonderland.

For all the remoteness of the location, there is plenty to do. Apart from the obvious pursuits such as hiking, fishing, quad-biking and heli-skiing, Takaro has an area for guests to immerse themselves in a rejuvenation of the mind and body. The high-ceilinged glass spa conveniently houses spa facilities such as a heated indoor pool, sauna and steam room.

A wide range of beauty and rejuvenation therapies is offered, including a five-person massage that has been rated by *Vogue* magazine as 'the best massage in the world' and is not to be missed. With its Life Design services, Takaro's Life Consultants will be on hand to answer all queries on health, rejuvenation, happiness, relationships, money, career or life itself. Together with the all-pervading sense of tranquillity, a dream-like and holistic state of rest and relaxation is all but guaranteed.

ROOMS
10 element-themed chalets •
6 traditional chalets

FOOD
gourmet restaurant: Western and Chinese

DRINK
bar

FEATURES
indoor pool • jacuzzi • steam room • sauna • massage • rejuvenation therapies • surround sound home theatre system • airfield • helipad • activity-booking service

BUSINESS
conference facilities • high-speed Internet access

NEARBY
Milford Sound • Doubtful Sound • glow-worm caves • hiking • fly- and spin-fishing • heli-skiing • quad-biking

CONTACT
914 Takaro Road, Te Anau 9640 • telephone: +64.3.249 0161 • facsimile: +64.3.249 0111 • email: contact@takarolodge.com • website: www.takarolodge.com

browns sotheby's international realty

With over 30 years of experience and deep local knowledge...

THIS PAGE (CLOCKWISE FROM RIGHT):
These luxury apartments offer generous views of Queenstown, Lake Wakatipu and The Remarkables mountain range; the eighth hole of the championship golf course at The Preserve at Jacks Point.

OPPOSITE (CLOCKWISE FROM TOP):
Fans of country living will relish Browns Sotheby's International Realty's offerings; the surrounding gardens are landscaped in tussock and rough boulders; an open concept allows the kitchen to integrate harmoniously into the living and dining areas.

Mention the name Sotheby's and some of the world's most remarkable auctions come to mind. Indeed, since 1744, Sotheby's has earned an exceptional reputation as a marketer for many of the most treasured and valuable possessions internationally. This impeccable reputation also extends to Sotheby's International Realty®, which boasts peerless connections and a far-reaching luxury real estate brokerage network spread over 350 offices in 20 countries.

Its New Zealand arm, Browns Sotheby's International Realty, is based in Queenstown. Like every international realty outpost of the group, it offers a wide range of unique and exclusive properties, from executive holiday homes to lifestyle holdings and town apartments.

Founded in May 2005 by Mark Harris, Michael Boulgaris and Julian and Nigel Brown, Browns Sotheby's International Realty focuses on the marketing of premium property. The Browns name has long been synonymous with the New Zealand property market. In fact, it was the Brown family who founded Queenstown Real Estate in 1973. With over 30 years of experience and deep local knowledge, they were naturals to tie up with Sotheby's International Realty®.

At the helm of International Business Development and Sales for Browns Sotheby's International Realty is Russell Reddell. A Queenstown resident since 1993, he has been a successful member of the local business community for over a decade. Extensive experience within the property market in Queenstown has allowed him to be personally involved with an array of lifestyle, development and investment properties. Together with a team of experienced property specialists, Russell helps to market properties in New Zealand for the wealthy and discerning.

Take, for instance, the Lake Ohau Station: a commanding presence in the majestic Southern Alps. One of New Zealand's largest privately owned properties since the 1950s, it was offered publicly for sale for the first time in 60 years. The sale was successfully managed by Russell of Browns Sotheby's International Realty.

Jacks Point in Queenstown is a newly established 1,214-hectare (3,000-acre) resort community. The Preserve at Jacks Point represents exclusive homesites set within the 18-hole championship golf course, with sweeping views of the lake and mountains. Here, Browns Sotheby's International Realty are the marketers for eight impressive sites ranging from 1 hectare to 1.7 hectares (2.5 acres to 4.2 acres). Ninety-five per cent of the land is dedicated to open spaces for native flora, walking trails and the golf course.

Equally awe-inspiring is the Pokapu residence. Set on 40 hectares (100 acres) of land, it looms large over Queenstown, endowing it with a panorama that never fails to impress. The construction of the 550-sq m (5,920-sq ft) house involved 1,740 tonnes (3,836,000 lbs) of concrete for the frame of the house alone. Inside, waxed concrete and schist complement the rugged terrain of the exterior.

Indeed, Browns Sotheby's International Realty takes its brand vision of 'artfully uniting extraordinary properties with extraordinary lives' seriously. After all, what good is a spectacular life if there isn't an equally amazing home to return to?

FEATURES
executive holiday homes • lifestyle holdings • town apartments

BUSINESS
real estate marketing

CONTACT
Russell Reddell,
International Business Development,
Browns Sotheby's International Realty,
Ground Floor, Sofitel, 8 Duke Street,
Queenstown 9300 •
telephone: +64.3.450 0483 •
facsimile: +64.3.450 0480 •
email: russell.reddell@sothebysrealty.com •
website: www.brownssothebysrealty.com

Browns Real Estate Ltd MREINZ
Each Office Is Independently Owned and Operated.

the villa book

...river stones...were handpicked to create the fireplace.

THIS PAGE (FROM ABOVE): *Maximising the lake and mountain views was a top priority for architect Brian Hollis; a gas fireplace and timber flooring enhance the living room, which is ideal for entertaining guests indoors.*
OPPOSITE (FROM RIGHT): *A fusion of Zen and New York styles enlivens the interior; a reflection of the modern Queenstown bedroom.*

A well-established and reliable property rental company, The Villa Book recognises the South Island as an ideal destination for a romantic retreat or family holiday.

One of its offerings is a property perched on the edge of Lake Wakatipu in Queenstown. Waking up to spectacular mornings is just one of the many delightful things about a stay here. Open your eyes to the sight of high mountain peaks set against a glimmering lake, catch the first rays of sun on the outdoor deck and end the day in the comfort of the private spa pool.

The property's architectural design is contemporary, with strategically placed windows that offer unsurpassed views of Lake Wakatipu, the Remarkables Mountain Range and Cecil Peak. Two apartments are available, one of which is an alluring penthouse. This house features a sprawling deck with a hot spa tub for eight, and an outdoor dining area with a large barbeque pit. The master bedroom's lavish en suite bathroom offers mountain vistas in an intimate setting. Wine aficionados will appreciate the wine cellar-cum-tasting room, while an entertainment and study area is equipped with the latest technology, from an integrated surround sound system to a card-swipe security system. In the kitchen, all the best appliances from Miele may inspire guests to prepare their own meals, especially since the kitchen was designed by New Zealand Designer of the Year, Lloyd Richardson.

A short drive will take guests to the international ski resorts of Queenstown or to verdant golf courses with rolling fairways. Not far from here also are Central Otago wineries and the World Heritage Fiordland National Park. Alternatively, the cosmopolitan city centre of Queenstown is a stone's throw away and lined with restaurants, cafés and the trendiest places to shop.

Queenstown is also the place for one of The Villa Book's most stylish apartments. Spread over three floors, its décor is classy, with beechwood panelling specially selected and milled for

the property. Indeed, impeccable attention to detail is visible in every aspect of this cavernous apartment, from the spacious black marble master bedroom en suite right down to the river stones that were handpicked to create the fireplace.

Its location in the heart of Queenstown translates to magical views across the bay and Lake Wakatipu. From the living area on the main level, guests can wander through the sliding doors and down to the courtyard garden that encloses a barbeque pit and plunge pool, which will be a treat for children. Like the rest of the apartment, the three bedrooms are exquisitely designed, with shades of dark chocolate against a smooth palette of cream, beech and white. Should the need arise, two extra guests can be comfortably accommodated in the study.

Naturally, the apartment comes with all the thoughtful touches which make it that much more special—climate-controlled underfloor heating and a state-of-the-art entertainment system which can be individually controlled from every room. Concierge service is also available, ensuring that the experience here leaves nothing to be desired.

THIS PAGE: In this Coronet Peak property, an open concept integrates the living, dining and kitchen areas, allowing guests to interact easily.

OPPPOSITE (CLOCKWISE FROM TOP): The dining room, with a high ceiling, seats eight comfortably; an enchanting view of the amber sunset and Lake Wanaka beckons; country-style architecture dominates the exterior.

Minutes from downtown Queenstown are the slopes of Coronet Peak, where The Villa Book's charming lodge sits along the road leading to the historic village of Arrowtown. Country-style meets luxurious, contemporary living, while old and new meld in the form of soft furnishings set against quality timber. In the living room, floor-to-ceiling windows render an airy feel, while a large open fire is the perfect place to cosy up to on winter nights. Large French doors open onto a quaint garden which entices guests to sit, relax and unwind. Upstairs, four large bedrooms offer queen-size beds, luxurious possum throws and dramatic views across the valley. In addition, a bunk-room further downstairs sleeps three.

Summer brings with it opportunities for peaceful walks through some of the most picturesque countryside in New Zealand. In winter, Coronet Peak, a skier's paradise, comes alive with ski pilgrims who spend all day on the slopes. Adventure-seekers will find plenty to do, with bungee jumping, river rafting and jet-boating being just some of the activities that will

get the adrenalin going. Guests who prefer a more sedate experience won't be disappointed either. They can take a leisurely boat trip across Lake Wakatipu or wander through the art galleries nearby. For all the other little luxuries, a concierge service can help arrange anything, from restaurant reservations to rejuvenating treatments at the in-house spa.

Further up north from Coronet Peak, set on 24 hectares (60 acres) of outstanding natural grounds, The Villa Book's property by the shores of Lake Wanaka offers fabulous views whichever way one turns. The lodge can house up to nine people (two double beds, two pairs of twins and one single). On one side the lake glimmers, while on the other, the snow-capped peaks of the Buchanan mountain range loom. Built in a traditional style and using natural materials, the house has a spacious open-concept living area which leads onto a verandah running the entire length of the property. Privacy is assured and even the secluded beaches, which are just a short stroll away, can be accessed only by a private road.

A vast lawn stretches towards the lake—the perfect spot for enjoying a glass of Central Otago Pinot Noir as the sun sets on the horizon. To ensure that there is something on the table for dinner, head out to the mouth of Matukituki River nearby, a well-known spot for trout fishing. Alternatively, to enjoy a complete gourmet feast, personal chefs are available upon request.

The town's attractions and activities are all within close proximity of the property, making it the ideal base from which to snowboard, heli-ski or windsurf, or simply do nothing at all.

FEATURES
all types of accommodation to suit various needs • private chefs

BUSINESS
villa rental

CONTACT
The Villa Book, 12 Venetian House, 47 Warrington Crescent, London W9 1EJ •
telephone: +44.845.500 2000 •
facsimile: +44.845.500 2001 •
email: info@thevillabook.com •
website: www.thevillabook.com

glacier southern lakes helicopters

A helicopter flight around New Zealand is like visiting 10 countries in a day.

Flying by helicopter is a thrilling sensation anywhere in the world, but to experience it in New Zealand? Well that's something very special indeed.

New Zealand is a land of spectacular contrasts with a landscape that comprises gentle greens of pastoral plains, crystal-clear lakes, blue crevasses of glaciers and jagged, snow-capped mountains. A helicopter flight around New Zealand is like visiting 10 countries in a day.

Glacier Southern Lakes Helicopters specialises in hosting guests on private charter excursions which may include fly-fishing for rainbow trout, snowmobiling in the back of beyond, jet-boating on isolated rivers, heli-skiing or boarding on private charters, hiking on glaciers or mountains, or simply enjoying the wonderful food and wine in Otago's breathtaking wilderness.

Glacier Southern Lakes Helicopters' team takes pride in delivering an exceptional flying experience. They are committed to exceeding passenger expectations and ensuring visitors take home unparalleled memories of the South Island, whether they have been flown to Milford and Doubtful Sounds, Stewart Island, Mount Cook or the glaciers at Fox and Franz Josef.

Based in Queenstown and founded in 1987, Glacier Southern Lakes Helicopters operates a fleet of modern four- and six-seater turbine helicopters whose experienced pilots offer vast local and regional knowledge while providing a professional and friendly service. They hold

THIS PAGE (CLOCKWISE FROM ABOVE):
Groups and private charters are a speciality, with glacier landings as an added thrill; Queenstown is more than just a base, offering many different sightseeing and adventure options.
OPPOSITE (FROM TOP): Milford and Doubtful Sounds should be on one's must-see list; landings in remote locations give travellers the opportunity to experience some of New Zealand's best-kept secrets.

PRODUCTS
scenic helicopter flights •
private charters

FEATURES
glacier landings • gourmet picnics •
concessions to land in exclusive areas •
flight options: heli-skiing, heli-fishing,
snowmobiling, heli-hiking and jet-boating

CONTACT
2 Lucas Place, PO Box 2152,
Queenstown 9349 •
telephone: +64.3.442 3016 •
facsimile: +64.3.442 3019 •
email: qtown@glaciersouthernlakes.co.nz •
website: www.glaciersouthernlakes.co.nz

concessions to land in exclusive terrain within the Fiordland National Park, providing passengers with a unique opportunity for exploration. Gourmet lunches accompanied by local wines can be enjoyed on a mountain top or at other locations where landing is permissible.

A wide selection of flight options will satisfy even the most discerning traveller, and these include scenic tours around the best of the South Island's scenery as well as combination trips offered in conjunction with some of Queenstown's best-known activity operators.

The renowned Milford Sound, often referred to as the 'Eighth Wonder of the World', is only thirty minutes by air from Queenstown and this exhilarating flight traverses the majestic Southern Alps into the lush green rainforest of Fiordland National Park. Passengers may stay awhile and experience a cruise on the fiord, or perhaps carry on via the Sutherland Falls, Lake Quill and Lake Manapouri to the quiet serenity of Doubtful Sound.

Visitors on a tight schedule needn't forego the South Island's famous landmarks, as Glacier Southern Lakes Helicopters offers a heli-tour which includes Mount Aspiring, Mount Cook, Mount Tasman and the West Coast glaciers, with a landing upon the mighty Fox Glacier.

And for an exclusive tour which few visitors are lucky enough to enjoy, take a spectacular flight over the southern part of the South Island: over Foveaux Strait and into Stewart Island's Rakiura National Park. Accompanied by professional guides, experience virgin forest, deserted beaches and well-formed walking tracks, and learn about the history, marine mammals and birdlife of this very special, remote part of New Zealand.

Travellers should make sure that they include a flight with Glacier Southern Lakes Helicopters on their South Island itinerary, as it promises to be the highlight of their Kiwi holiday.

food+wine

North Cape
Three Kings Islands

North Island

▲ 770 ● **Whangarei**

Great Barrier Island

> Kumeu River Wines
> The French Café
> Villa Maria Estate   ○ Takapuna
> Cibo Restaurant   **Auckland** ✈
> Antoine's Restaurant   Manukau
> Antipodes Water
> White Restaurant at Hilton Auckland

East Cape

Hamilton ●   ✈ **Tauranga**

○ Wakatane ▲ 1754

Taupo ○   **Gisborne** ✈   > The Millton Vineyard
                                      > The Wharf Café, Bar + Restaurant
New Plymouth ● ✈   > Craggy Range Winery + Terrôir Restaurant

▲ 2518   ▲ 2797

                        ● **Napier**
Wanganui ○   Hastings ○
             ▲ 1733

Feilding ○   ● **Palmerston North**

○ Levin
             ✈

**Tasman
Sea**

Collingwood ●

                ▲ 1209   Upper
> Neudorf Vineyards   Hutt ○   ○ Masterton
> Hopgood's Restaurant + Bar   **Nelson** ● Lower Hutt   > Ata Rangi
> Nautilus Estate of Marlborough **Blenheim** ■ **Wellington** > Saluté Restaurant
                    ▲ 1875   > Palliser Estate Wines of Martinborough
                                                    > Boulcott Street Bistro
                ▲ 2339   ▲ 2885   > Fromm Winery La Strada
                        ▲ 2160   > Gibb's Vineyard Restaurant
                                                    > Lawson's Dry Hills
Greymouth ●   > Herzog Luxury Restaurant

        ▲ 2400

      ▲ 2795   > Pegasus Bay Winery
▲ 3764   ✈   > Pescatore Restaurant
      Christchurch ●

**South
Island**   Ashburton ○

**South
Pacific
Ocean**

▲ 3027   Chatham Islands
▲ 2745   ▲ 1910 ○ Timaru

▲ 2131   ▲ 2134   Pitt Island
      ▲ 2324 ▲ 1643   > The Postmaster's House Restaurant
Queenstown ●   > Felton Road
▲ 1853   Oamaru ○

      ▲ 1450

● **Dunedin**

▲ 1189

✈ **Invercargill**

Foveaux Strait
      ▲ 980
Stewart Island

South Cape

Legend
═ Highway
▬ Main Road
✈ Airport
   Water
● 3000–4000 m
● 2000–3000 m
● 1000–2000 m
● 500–1000 m
● 200–500 m

N
↑

0 km   60   120   180 km

food, glorious food

New Zealand is a gastronomic goldmine, with a growing reputation not only for its award-winning wines, but also for its fresh produce, superb cafés, restaurants and eateries. The food scene in New Zealand has changed dramatically over the past twenty years; its current cuisine-orientated culture has created a generation of appreciative consumers and innovative providers. Rich in basic ingredients, New Zealand has been blessed with tasty produce. Its offering of seafood is a delicious mix of fresh fish, gigantic crayfish, succulent scallops and the famous Green-lipped mussels and Bluff oysters. The New Zealand lamb is known worldwide for its unique flavour, and the fruit and vegetables cultivated in New Zealand have the advantage of being raised in an environment conducive to both growth and taste. With ingredients of such high standard on offer, New Zealand has made the world take note of its gastronomic revolution, and this has placed New Zealand firmly on the culinary map.

all in the mix

A number of high-profile chefs from New Zealand have made their mark; some are internationally acclaimed, while others are more recognised on home territory. To name a few: Peter Gordon, who was born in the coastal town of Wanganui, is best known for his fusion style, and he has restaurants in both Auckland and London. Charles Royal, a pioneer of traditional native cuisine, has worked closely with Air New Zealand to introduce traditional flavours to its in-flight menus. Simon Gault is considered to be one of the country's most outstanding chefs, while the flamboyant Peta Mathias is a household name in New Zealand. Exceeding the exacting demands of international fine dining standards for local cuisine, there is an abundance of cultural influences at work, springing from the melting pot of nationalities in New Zealand. From Mediterranean to Pacific to Asian, the myriad of cooking styles that have been added into the mix have influenced every form of dining available.

PAGE 174: *New Zealand pumpkins and butternut squash are incorporated into many dishes from salads to sandwiches.*

THIS PAGE: *Green-lipped mussels are just one of the many culinary experiences visitors will enjoy. Large, fleshy and with their own distinctive flavour, they are delicious.*

OPPOSITE: *A winery at the foot of the mountains in Queenstown.*

global growth

Local chefs, who have in the past looked overseas for global inspiration, are now also turning to their own culture and making use of the country's natural resources. Increasingly, native herbs, such as kawakawa, horopito and piko piko, have been introduced into menus, with an array of spices and seasonings used in both traditional and contemporary dishes. Because of this trend, food enthusiasts have been inspired to start producing their own raw materials, as opposed to importing them from overseas. All kinds of 'homegrown' ingredients have become available, many with a Kiwi twist. Consumers now have access to everything from delicious New Zealand avocado oils to saffron and vanilla.

Such innovation is not merely confined to food: a New Zealand-produced premium vodka has taken the international market by storm with its refreshing taste and exotic flavours, such as Feijoa, Manuka Honey and Kiwifruit. Less grandiose in scale of production, but by no means any less inventive or delicious, are the numerous niche gourmet delicacies found at farmers' markets or distributed by small suppliers.

From cheeses to chutneys, many of these delicacies have caught the attention of restaurant owners. In a recent trend, chefs from abroad have started to come to New Zealand to scour these outlets for exciting new finds. It is increasingly becoming the case where it is not just the basic, traditional produce which is being exported, but also the homemade delicacies as well. Today, a large number of speciality food manufacturers supply produce like cheese, honey, ice-cream and other gourmet items for local and overseas consumers.

the tastes of home

In many homes, cooking styles hark back to their immigrant roots: new arrivals from Europe after the Second World War introduced different flavours and food products. Given a predominance of British descendants, it is little surprise that the traditional roast dinner is a well-loved dish. However, the side servings add a Pacific feel— pumpkin and kumara (sweet potato) are usually roasted alongside potatoes. No Kiwi kitchen is complete without a copy of the country's most iconic recipe book, the *Edmonds Cookery Book*, which is filled with recipes most families have grown up with. Treasured dishes include the Bacon and Egg Pie, a puff pastry casing filled with eggs, topped with bacon and cooked to high temperatures, and Whitebait Fritters, a dish prepared from egg and tiny whitebait.

The most famous New Zealand dessert is the pavlova, a crispy meringue that melts in the mouth and comes laden with fruit and cream. Other popular sweet treats include banana cake, date scones, pikelets, Anzac biscuits, Afghan cookies and muffins.

Although essentially a nation of meat lovers, vegetables feature strongly on any menu, with local markets and vegetable stores offering extensive choices. Regional options are often dependent on local harvests. The subtropical climate allows a number of exciting fruit and vegetables to flourish. In addition to the standard pip fruits, plenty of other fruit varieties thrive; these include tamarillos, persimmons, pepinos, feijoas and avocados. These exotic fruits serve as a small reminder of New Zealand's South Pacific location.

THIS PAGE (FROM TOP): Believed to have been originally created in New Zealand, the pavlova is traditionally decorated with whipped cream and fresh fruit; the regional food and wine of New Zealand often complement each other to perfection.

OPPOSITE: Food constitutes a big part of a visit to New Zealand. Whether travellers prefer a meal in a world-class restaurant or in a winery, they will find that this is all part of the journey of discovery.

eat in, take away

One of the most popular take-away foods is the savoury pie. Considered to be an intrinsic part of a New Zealander's diet, the range of flavours encompasses everything from potato-topped mince (or steak) and cheese, to seafood or vegetable. Of course, another big love is the fish-and-chip supper, with side orders such as battered oysters and scallops often added to the standard repertoire.

Coffee is big business in New Zealand, and many cafés are proud of the quality of their beans and the extent of their selection. With little in the way of pre-packaged lunch foods, cafés tend to provide extensive choices. Most will offer a range of salads, and an array of sandwich fillings served in speciality breads such as wraps, ciabatta, focaccia or panini. Quiches, frittatas and 'stacks' are also mainstays. A café's cake counter is a further adventure for the diner, usually featuring oversized wedges of cake and mammoth muffins.

hot stuff

In many homes, food preparation largely revolves around the barbecue. Indeed, there is no meal which cannot be prepared on the barbecue grill. From scrambled eggs to the finest beef fillet, there is no doubt that barbecued fare is an art form in this country. However, the most traditional way to prepare a meal (one which is still used across New Zealand, although most usually on special occasions) is the Maori hangi, or earth oven. Meat and vegetables are packed into baskets and steamed over hot rocks in a covered pit; the result is a wonderfully tender and flavoursome feast that can feed a large number of people. While the food is made ready in the same way as if to be cooked in an ordinary oven, a hangi can be quite time consuming as there is a good deal of preparatory work involved.

THIS PAGE (FROM TOP): In a café in Wellington. The café culture has evolved to become an integral part of New Zealand life; a barbecue is an intrinsic part of the cooking process in New Zealand, and can be enjoyed at home, in the park or on a beach.

OPPOSITE: In anticipation of a meal aboard a luxury yacht.

liquid delight

While the food is sublime, it is the wine from New Zealand which first caught the attention of the outside world. New Zealand is renowned for producing world-class vintages. However, the relatively new discovery of New Zealand wine can be attributed to its recent history of wine-making and the fact that it took until the 1970–80s before New Zealand found its niche. It was in 1974 when the first Sauvignon Blanc was produced near Auckland. In subsequent years, wine-makers began to concentrate their efforts on white wines like the Sauvignon Blanc and Chardonnay. So successful were these efforts that the Sauvignon Blanc is now seen as the signature wine of New Zealand, although of late, Pinot Noir is proving to be another excellent choice.

grape expectations

New Zealand has been experimenting and producing wine since the early days of European colonisation. By all accounts, the grape vine was introduced in 1819. However, James Busby, who was also the author of the Treaty of Waitangi, is New Zealand's first recorded wine-maker, having planted a vineyard on his Waitangi estate in the Bay of Islands in 1834. Busby was no stranger to wine-making—he not only studied it, but also helped to establish the wine industry in New South Wales, Australia.

The wines which he produced on his Northland property were sampled by the French admiral Dumont d'Urville, who was extremely complimentary about Busby's efforts.

In the South Island, French settlers planted small vineyards in Akaroa. However, it is in Hawke's Bay, New Zealand's best-known wine-producing area, and the Auckland-Northland region, that small commercial vineyards began to spring up by the close of the century. Over the years, immigrants brought with them different varieties of grapes which were dutifully tried, tested and experimented with. Among the pioneers were the Dalmatian Croats who settled in the Auckland region.

It was during the 1960s when wine-making experimentation really started in earnest. Unfortunately, a number of less-than-scintillating wines was the result, and it wasn't until the creation of the Sauvignon Blanc that wide-scale success was achieved.

a very special blend

New Zealand is a prime territory for wine production, with most of the vineyards planted on the east coast away from the prevailing westerly winds on flat, eroded river deltas and valleys. The vintages produced on the east coast have their own distinctive and unique flavour. A considerable number of grape varieties are grown across an expansive countryside that shows definite regional characteristics. Thus, it is hard to generalise the taste of New Zealand wine. However, it is fair to say that these wines reflect their maritime, cool-climate origin. Descriptive terms often applied to the wines are 'intense', 'crisp', 'zesty', 'lively', and on occasion, 'exceptionally fruity'; all have been used to surmise the attributes of the wine.

In New Zealand, there is an inclination towards grape varieties that thrive in cooler climes and relatively infertile soil types, such as the aforementioned Sauvignon Blanc, Chardonnay and Pinot Noir. The more subtropical parts of the country—mainly in the North Island—have had success with grapes suited to warmer conditions. Some examples are the Cabernet Sauvignon and Syrah. Generally, the growing season begins in September, with harvesting taking place between February and April.

THIS PAGE: *Diners having a meal at Pegasus Bay, a family-owned and operated winery and restaurant in Waipara, North Canterbury.*

OPPOSITE (FROM LEFT): *Rows of empty wine bottles; a winery in Hawke's Bay noted for its red wines, Chardonnays and Sauvignon Blancs.*

regional tendencies

Generally speaking, Hawke's Bay is seen as home to household wines such as Merlot, Cabernet Sauvignon and Syrah, which are all varieties that enjoy the warm maritime climate of the area. Gisborne is a smaller, but still renowned wine-producing region, and here the pick would be the full-bodied Chardonnays.

At the bottom of the North Island is the Wairarapa/Martinborough region, the latter being one of New Zealand's premier wine regions despite its small size. Wairarapa is considered a 'newbie' to the wine industry, but it has seen rapid growth over the last 20 years. A popular day-trip from Wellington, these two regions regularly attract visitors with their Pinot Noirs, Riesling, Pinot Gris, Chardonnay and Gewurztraminer wines. In the warmer northern areas, Waikato and the Bay of Plenty err towards Chardonnays, while the Auckland area is primarily a red wine zone, concentrating on the production of Cabernet Sauvignon. Northland also tends to specialise in red wines such as the Merlot.

In the South Island, Marlborough is an extensive and exquisite area for wine production. The majority of its vineyards can be found around Renwick, Blenheim and Cloudy Bay in the Wairau valley. Warm days and cool nights breed a beautiful Sauvignon Blanc, as well as some Chardonnay and other sparkling wines. Indeed, many critics consider this region to produce the world's best Sauvignon Blanc. Central Otago is a sheltered inland area; its vineyards are also the highest in New Zealand, rising 200 m to 400 m (656 ft to 1,312 ft) above sea level. Because of its extreme southerly position, the growing season in Central Otago is short, but still long enough to produce a phenomenal Pinot Noir, which is the leading grape variety in the region and accounts for about 70 per cent of the plantings there.

THIS PAGE (FROM TOP): Although screw tops are now par for course, it is still possible to find corks used in bottles of wines; a waiter preparing the scene for a wine-tasting session.
OPPOSITE: Barrels lined up in the cellar exude the heady scent of the wine held within.
PAGE 186: Vineyard after snowfall during the winter season.

New Zealand is a prime territory for wine production...

the family of twelve

...their strong passion and dedication towards making high-quality artisanal wine...

THIS PAGE: *The Family of Twelve (from left to right)—Paul Brajkovich, Ivan Donaldson, Judy Finn, Steve Smith, Phyll Pattie, Richard Riddiford, Clive Weston, Ross Lawson, Annie Millton, Blair Walter, Pol Lenzinger and George Fistonich.*

OPPOSITE (CLOCKWISE FROM TOP): *Red grapes are harvested for the production of Pinot Noir, one of New Zealand's dominant wines; curling tendrils of the vines; the wineries each have their own specialities but with perfection as their common goal, all produce award-winning wines.*

There is a family of wineries in New Zealand that's like no other. The common thread that binds all 12 together is their strong passion and dedication towards making high-quality artisanal wine for both local and international enthusiasts. Their passion does not stop with their own wineries, rather it unfolds into the whole New Zealand wine industry.

Formed in 2003, The Family of Twelve comprises wine-producers spanning different regions of New Zealand, a land of extremes and home to the world's most easterly and most southerly vineyards. The Family's wines are created using a wide range of grape varieties grown in the country, from Sauvignon Blanc to Pinot Noir, from Gewürztraminer to Syrah. Six of the wineries are located in New Zealand's North Island; Kumeu River Wines and Villa Maria Estate in Auckland; The Millton Vineyard in Gisborne; Craggy Range Winery in Hawkes Bay; Palliser Estate and Ata Rangi in Martinborough. The other six are from the South Island: Fromm Winery, Nautilus Estate and Lawson's Dry Hills in Marlborough; Neudorf Vineyards in Nelson; Pegasus Bay Winery in Waipara and Felton Road in Central Otago.

These artisan wine-makers are united as producers of premium individual wines and, working as an export alliance, the family's collective drive is to promote quality New Zealand wine to both well-established and newly emerging markets around the world.

The members of The Family of Twelve are all top producers in their own right, and all manage to express their own individuality through their wine. Made up of Kiwis, Dalmatians, Australians, English and Swiss, they proudly identify themselves as New Zealanders. Producing award-winning labels that are consistently successful in both national and international competitions and in gaining accolades from various magazine reviews, all have made a mark on the international scene with well-established distribution channels. By maintaining their high standards of producing exceptional wines, the world stage is where The Family of Twelve is and where it will undoubtedly stay.

The love and appreciation of their authentic experience is what drives them. Knowing that a family is behind the label, with real people who are passionate about what they do makes their wines all the more superior. Thankfully, for wine-lovers around the world, these top New Zealand wines are evidently in good hands and, if great wine is achieved when it is an expression of the vineyard, the land and the people, then The Family of Twelve is on the right track to achieving its goal year after year.

CONTACT
email: familyofxii@xtra.co.nz •
website: www.familyoftwelve.co.nz

ata rangi + saluté restaurant

...a leading New World producer of Pinot Noir.

Ata Rangi means 'new beginning' or literally, 'dawn sky'. It is an apt name for a vineyard that has flourished so brightly over the years. In 1980, Clive Paton bought and planted the original, barren, 5-hectare (12-acre) home paddock at the edge of a Martinborough village, then a forgotten rural settlement in the lower North Island. In doing so, he became one of a handful of people who pioneered grape-growing in the region.

Having farmed in the area, Clive knew the land and its elements well. Based on his knowledge, he chose to plant mainly red varieties with the aim of producing world-class wines. Almost 30 years later and still proudly family-owned, Ata Rangi is considered a leading New World producer of Pinot Noir. Along the way, the team has picked up a string of national and international trophies, including the coveted Bouchard-Finlayson trophy thrice for 'Best Pinot Noir' at the International Wine and Spirit Competition.

One of their more recent releases of Pinot Noir is from the outstanding 2006 vintage. Rich with dark plum and cherry, it also has delicate spicy undertones and a hint of deftly handled oak. With persistent silky tannins running right through the wine, it has all the qualities that promise a wine which will improve for at least seven years.

THIS PAGE (CLOCKWISE FROM ABOVE):
Storing Ata Rangi's renowned wines, these wooden boxes are used to distribute the wines both locally and internationally; encouraging biodiversity, wildflowers abound in Ata Rangi vineyards in spring.

OPPOSITE (CLOCKWISE FROM TOP):
Ata Rangi Pinot Noir is favoured for its texture and pure fruit expression; cinnamon is frequently used in Saluté's cuisine; Saluté's menu offers stylish, aromatic and contemporary cuisine inspired by the flavours of North Africa and the Middle East.

The year 2006 was also exceptional for Ata Rangi Craighall Chardonnay and their Lismore Pinot Gris. These are all serious, hand-crafted wines, aromatic and beautifully balanced with a texture and structure that complements perfectly the fragrant, contemporary Middle Eastern cuisine of Saluté restaurant in the nearby village of Greytown. With a reputation for superb food, wine

and service, and twice finalist in *Cuisine*'s New Zealand Restaurant of the Year Awards, Saluté attracts not only locals but also regular visitors from the capital city of Wellington.

Owner and talented chef Travis Clive-Griffin has worked with some of the most highly regarded chefs in Australia and the UK, including Jacques Reymond, Stephanie Alexander and Raymond Blanc. His relationship with Middle Eastern food started as a young boy in the kitchen of his Lebanese grandfather. At Saluté, Travis widely uses the vibrant, sweet spice flavours of the Middle East and North Africa. Think of saffron, cumin, coriander, cardamom,

paprika and a plethora of locally grown fresh herbs. The robust dishes that result pair perfectly with the region's wines and those of Ata Rangi in particular. Travis' irresistible risotto is prepared with porcini and 'Ras El Hanout' roasted duck, with caramelised onions and wild thyme, topped with duck crackling. The dish is best paired with Ata Rangi Pinot Noir.

With lunchtime al fresco seating in the shady courtyard, complete with trees and a fountain, or indoor dining enhanced by a warm décor and personalised service, it is no wonder Saluté enjoys so many loyal clientele and is regularly filled to capacity.

Ata Rangi

PRODUCTS
Pinot Noir • Chardonnay • Sauvignon Blanc • Pinot Gris

FEATURE
wine-tasting

NEARBY
Martinborough Village

CONTACT
Ata Rangi, Puruatanga Road, PO Box 43, Martinborough 5741 • telephone: +64.3.306 9570 • facsimile: +64.3.306 9523 • email: wines@atarangi.co.nz • website: www.atarangi.co.nz

Saluté Restaurant

SEATS
dining area: 65 • al fresco area: 65

FOOD
contemporary Middle Eastern

DRINK
Old and New World wines • cocktails

FEATURE
courtyard with fountain

CONTACT
83 Main Street, Greytown 5953 • telephone: +64.6.304 9825 • facsimile: +64.6.304 9829 • email: reservations@salute.greytown.co.nz • website: www.salute.greytown.co.nz

craggy range winery + terrôir restaurant

...New Zealand's answer to the Médoc.

THIS PAGE (CLOCKWISE FROM ABOVE):
Early morning mist fills the
air around the Giants;
an enchanting view of
Terrôir from across the lake;
a meandering path cuts
across the vineyard, which
is rich in alluvial soil.
OPPOSITE (FROM TOP): Rabbit Terrine
with Tamarillo Relish;
the restaurant frequently
draws a full house.

Craggy Range's home, known as the Giants Winery, is one of New Zealand's most ambitious to date. Run by the dynamic Terry Peabody and Steve Smith MW, the Craggy Range philosophy is 'Single Vineyard, Single Minded'. Their idea is to select the top vineyards in the country, plant them with vines which are appropriate for the particular terroir and bottle them as single-estate wines.

Inspired by the agricultural heritage of New Zealand and the glamour of Bordeaux, architect John Blair created a serene patchwork of lakes, lawns, vines and winery buildings against the awe-inspiring backdrop of Te Mata Peak. Travellers could not hope for a more harmonious environment in which to enjoy these finely crafted wines. The estate spans a total of 185 hectares (457 acres) in Martinborough and the niche Gimblett Gravels region of Hawkes Bay, a stony terroir with a reputation as New Zealand's answer to the Médoc.

Very few vineyards have an in-house Master of Wine, but Craggy Range does, in the form of Steve Smith, a producer of expressive single-estate Sauvignons and Bordeaux-styled reds. World wine authority Robert Parker calls his Le Sol Syrah 2002 one of the finest reds he has ever tasted from New Zealand. Steve's wines have also received praise from the respected wine magazine *Decanter*. Guests visiting this cutting-edge winery will soon understand just what it is that makes this New World destination such a viticultural favourite.

Suitable for a private wine-tasting session, the Quarry Cellar is conveniently located just beneath the winery. A tour of the cellar highlights the impeccable quality of these wines through an explanation of the typical processes involved in wine-making. Hundreds of purpose-built tanks and French oak barrels disappear into beautifully lit alcoves with mosaic-tiled floors. Each contains an individual parcel of wine, vinified separately to preserve its unique flavours.

After this evocative tour, the estate's country French-themed Terrôir restaurant is just the place to savour the stunning wines of Craggy Range. New Zealand's 'Sommelier of the Year 2006', Matt Judd, is on hand to assist visitors in wine selection. With its rustic ambience, Terrôir's dining experience is dubbed by *Condé Nast Traveler* as close to perfection.

Located right beneath the breathtaking peak of Te Mata, the kitchen at Terrôir is headed by Executive Chef Stephen Tindall, who specialises in rotisserie and wood-fired oven cooking. He is known for using succulent cuts of meat and fresh, local seafood in his menu.

Sample the Herb-Stuffed Crisp Pork Belly with Savoy Cabbage, Pistachio, Peach and Pomegranate Relish and complement it with Craggy Range's Te Muna Vineyard Pinot Noir 2005. Alternatively, match the creamy textures of the winery's C3 Chardonnay Hawkes Bay with the White Wine Marinated Rotisserie Chicken with Whole Roasted Mushroom, Aioli and Pine Nuts. For a heartier dish, the Awanui Beef Fillet has a pepper-crusted spiciness which is best paired with Craggy Range's Sophia from the Gimblett Gravels region.

Craggy Range excels in blending tradition with innovation, art with technology and the best French cuisine with the finest local wines. Leaving New Zealand without tasting its magical combination of food and wine will be a huge miss for connoisseurs.

Craggy Range Winery

PRODUCTS
Gimblett Gravels Syrah, Merlot and Cabernet • Hawkes Bay Chardonnay • Marlborough and Martinborough Sauvignon Blanc • Central Otago and Martinborough Pinot Noir • Waipara Riesling

FEATURES
cellar door • The Cellar Master's Cottage • winery tours

NEARBY
art galleries • museums • trout fishing • jet tours • mountain biking

CONTACT
253 Waimarama Road, Havelock North, Hawkes Bay 4230 • telephone: +64.6.873 7126 • facsimile: +64.6.873 7141 • email: info@craggyrange.com • website: www.craggyrange.com

Terrôir Restaurant

SEATS
main dining area: 110 • al fresco area: 80

FOOD
traditional French

DRINK
single-vineyard wines from Craggy Range • international wine list

FEATURES
lake and mountain views

CONTACT
253 Waimarama Road, Havelock North, Hawkes Bay 4230 • telephone: +64.6.873 0143 • email: info@craggyrange.com • website: www.craggyrange.com

felton road +
the postmaster's house restaurant

...created with the refined skills of an alchemist.

THIS PAGE (FROM TOP): With north-facing slopes, Felton Road's original vineyard, Elms, is ideal for grape-growing; the winery's main building exudes a rustic feel; harvesting by hand begins in early April.

OPPOSITE (FROM TOP): Dine in a romantic atmosphere by the warm fireplace; The Postmaster's House Restaurant—one of the distinct icons in Arrowtown; a blend of Felton Road's vineyards: Elms, Cornish Point and Calvert, creates this multi-layered Pinot Noir.

Bannockburn in Central Otago may be the perfect place to explore New Zealand's gold-mining history. But having the world's most southerly vineyards at a latitude of 45 degrees south, its reputation as the fine wine-growing region of the future is eclipsing its industrial past.

One of the southern hemisphere's most talked-about wineries, Felton Road produces wines which are on par with Burgundy's and California's finest. Wine-maker Blair Walter's exemplary Pinot Noir, Riesling and Chardonnay are created with the refined skills of an alchemist. Critics such as Britain's Oz Clarke (*Pocket Wine Book*) and Robert Parker (*The Wine Advocate*) sang praises for his work, the latter describing Felton Road's Pinot Noir as 'breakthrough efforts in New Zealand'.

With low rainfall, long periods of sunlight and a dramatic setting, Felton Road was quick to plant its first of three vineyards, Elms, in these spectacular surroundings in 1992. Strategically located in a microclimate environment and on the gentle north-facing valley, the site for Elms is indeed conducive to the production of world-class wines. This vineyard today is planted with Pinot Noir, Chardonnay and Riesling for the estate's principal wines. In addition, the gently oaked wines are aged in barrels crafted by some of Burgundy's top coopers. The panorama of Felton Road's second vineyard, Cornish Point, is an unforgettable sight, with dawn mists rising from the river and snow-capped mountains forming a fitting backdrop. It would come as no surprise if New Zealand's moniker as the 'Land of the Long White Cloud' were derived from this picturesque landscape.

To understand and appreciate the allure of Felton Road's wines, visitors are encouraged to attend an informative tasting session at Felton Road. Alternatively, detour to Arrowtown for a visit to The Postmaster's House Restaurant. Finalist in *Cuisine*'s Restaurant of the Year in 2005 and 2006, the *New York Times* describes its ambience, service and cuisine as 'almost perfect'.

Housed in a historic wooden cottage just 20 minutes from Queenstown, the restaurant's innovative menu showcases the freshest local harvest. This inclination towards providing a first-class experience for guests extends to the

formidable wine list, which represents owner Peter Waters' passion for premium, cool-climate wines. Peter suggests Felton Road's aromatic 2005 Riesling alongside the Karaage Style West Coast Whitebait with Tamarind and Palm Sugar Dressing. The delicate aroma of the fish is enhanced by the pure, piercing acidity of this noble wine.

Aficionados of red wine will appreciate the chemistry between a generous glass of Felton Road's Pinot Noir and the restaurant's signature dish, Pan-Seared Wild Fiordland Venison with dark plum jus, hazelnut and caper biscotti.

A select bottle from Felton Road's single-vineyard 'Block' range will inspire a second visit to the region of Central Otago, even before the first glass is finished. Capturing the essence of each vineyard, these eloquent, expressive wines are a superb introduction to the impressive portfolio of Felton Road.

Felton Road

PRODUCTS
single-vineyard 'Block' range:
Pinot Noir • Chardonnay • Riesling

FEATURES
wine-tasting • mountain views

NEARBY
horse riding • fishing • hiking •
cultural tours • gold-mining heritage

CONTACT
Bannockburn, RD 2, Central Otago
9384 • telephone: +64.3.445 0885 •
facsimile: +64.3.445 0881 •
email: wines@feltonroad.com •
website: www.feltonroad.com

The Postmaster's House Restaurant

SEATS
dining area: 40 •
outdoor cocktail area: 100

FOOD
contemporary French and Asian

DRINK
bar • extensive wine list • cocktails

FEATURES
cottage • garden •
catering for special events

CONTACT
54 Buckingham Street,
Arrowtown, Central Otago 9302 •
telephone: +64.3.442 0991 •
facsimile: +64.3.442 0983 • email:
bookings@postmastershouse.com •
website: www.postmastershouse.com

fromm winery la strada + gibb's vineyard restaurant

...there isn't a weak wine in Fromm's elaborate portfolio.

A boutique winery with a focus on handcrafted, quality wines, Fromm Winery La Strada has become one of New Zealand's most exciting producers within one generation. Master of Wine Bob Campbell once said that his dying wish would be for a taste of Fromm's seductively-silken La Strada Pinot Noir—in double magnum.

In 1992, George Fromm left his vineyard in Switzerland to begin his Marlborough adventure on the northeastern tip of the South Island. Today, successful entrepreneur Pol Lenzinger joins him. In a region known for reputable New World whites, Fromm stands out as its first red wine pioneer. A role model for New Zealand wine, even its competitors will admit there isn't a weak wine in Fromm's elaborate portfolio.

The cedar-clad, down-to-earth winery is reached via a tree-lined drive. Surrounded by orderly close-planted vines, its architecture reflects the delicate balance of class and understatement, something similarly present in wine-making. The cellar door allows visitors to experience what it takes to produce Fromm's wines through comprehensive wine-tastings in the immediate vicinity of the working winery.

The establishment's low-alcohol Rieslings have developed a loyal following far beyond its boundaries as has its prestigious Pinot Noir, more reminiscent of Burgundy than the New World. Aged in French oak barrels, each bottle has structure, elegance, complexity and above all, a fine texture. This makes for great food wines. Fromm Pinot Noir 94 Reserve was the first significant Pinot. It excelled in comparative tastings, putting the winery on the world map. This high standard has been attained by the winery's subsequent vintages as well.

Fromm's intuitive wine-makers Hatsch Kalberer and William Hoare believe in the essence of Old World viticulture and wine-making tradition. Their philosophy places terroir over technology, and grape quality over quantity. They are dedicated to producing intense, concentrated wines that proudly proclaim their origin. Their passion extends to cultivating Merlot, Malbec, Pinot Noir and mineral scented Chardonnay.

A natural progression from an informative and enjoyable winery visit is a trip to Gibb's Vineyard Restaurant, located in nearby Blenheim. Run by Heidi and

THIS PAGE (FROM ABOVE): *A scenic view of Fromm's vineyard in Blenheim; the winery is set against a backdrop of verdant mountains.*

OPPOSITE (CLOCKWISE FROM TOP): *Fromm's Pinot Noir has gained worldwide recognition; Rack of Lamb and Pan Fried Tenderloin of Veal are highlights in Gibb's menu; the restaurant has a homely, European feel.*

Chris Gibb, this is vineyard dining at its best. The innovative menu is designed with European flair and an emphasis on simple, pure flavours.

The unpretentious cottage, which the restaurant is housed in, has a casual yet stylish interior, with exposed beams and colourful artwork on the walls. Light and spacious, it boasts a comprehensive wine list of Marlborough's best estates and New Zealand's top wines. Needless to say, Fromm wines feature prominently.

Gibb's signature dish is Rack of Lamb, rubbed in mustard and fresh herbs, with roasted vegetables and creamy silverbeet. Tease the best out of this mouth-watering dish with a cellared vintage of Fromm Vineyard Pinot Noir. Alternatively, an appetising white such as an elegant Clayvin Vineyard Chardonnay complements the fresh 'catch of the day'. Desserts exude a European flair, with Streuselkuchen (almond-crusted apricot tart), Lime Panna Cotta and Belgian Chocolate Mousse oozing with appeal.

After days spent hiking or driving across New Zealand, a little self-indulgence is justified. Set aside a day of luxury to taste the top-class wines of Fromm Winery La Strada and to meet Heidi and Chris at their charming Gibb's Vineyard Restaurant.

Fromm Winery La Strada

PRODUCTS
Riesling • Chardonnay • Pinot Noir • Merlot • Malbec • Syrah • Gewürztraminer

FEATURES
cellar door

NEARBY
four-wheel drive tours • arts and crafts • bird watching • lake cruises • mountain biking • diving • trekking

CONTACT
Godfrey Road, RD 2, Blenheim 7272, Marlborough •
telephone: +64.3.572 9355 •
facsimile: +64.3.572 9366 •
email: lastrada@frommwineries.com •
website: www.frommwineries.com

Gibb's Vineyard Restaurant

SEATS
dining area: 50 • al fresco area: 80

FOOD
seasonal European

DRINK
New Zealand wines

FEATURES
summer Bierfest event • catering service • wine-and-dine dinners

CONTACT
258 Jacksons Road, RD 3, Blenheim 7273, Marlborough •
telephone: +64.3.572 8048 •
facsimile: +64.3.572 8048 •
email: info@gibbs-restaurant.co.nz •
website: www.gibbs-restaurant.co.nz

kumeu river wines + the french café

...most famous for its Chardonnay...

THIS PAGE (CLOCKWISE FROM RIGHT): The winery was built in 1948, but still retains its original character to this day; Kumeu River's Pinot Gris; the vineyard in autumn produces bright hues of orange and yellow.

OPPOSITE (FROM TOP): Each oak barrel has its unique stamp of identification; The French Café's sophisticated brown furniture contrasts well with the ivory-themed interior décor.

In 1938, Mick and Kate Brajkovich arrived from the Dalmatian Coast and worked in the Gum fields in Northland before saving enough money to buy their own land in Kumeu, just north of Auckland in 1944. Their son Mate, then 18, became well-known in the area and later a prominent figure in New Zealand's wine-making history. Known as Kumeu River Wines, this family winery is now run by Mate's wife, Melba, and their four children, Michael, Marijana, Milan and Paul. Melba can often be seen talking to customers in the winery's cellar door shop.

Kumeu River is most famous for its Chardonnay. This wine has been compared to fine Meursault and is revered for having the characters of 'white Burgundy, not simple Chardonnay'. Earning consistently high scores in *Wine Spectator* magazine, the Chardonnay has made it to the annual top 100 in the magazine on six occasions.

Mate's son, Michael, is Kumeu River's wine-maker and was the first New Zealander to become a Master of Wine when he passed the rigorous Institute of Masters of Wine examinations in 1989.

Michael's international experience led him to develop the first-class Kumeu River range in 1983 which now includes the Chardonnay, Pinot Gris, Pinot Noir and Merlot.

Savour Kumeu River wines in Auckland's The French Café. This sophisticated, pristine white venue is *Cuisine*'s 'Restaurant of the Year' 2006, topping many fine dining polls. Enjoy an aperitif in the courtyard or bar before proceeding with an intimate dinner for two or a spontaneous social gathering.

Owner Simon Wright has established his name in Europe's top Michelin-starred restaurants. A master craftsman, his menus showcase the best seasonal produce available. The Café's award-winning staff will expertly pair any of its contemporary European dishes with its perfect match on the wine list, which spans the best of Australasia and France.

Patrons are advised to pair the Roasted Crayfish Tail with Sweet Carrot Purée, Almond Foam, Baby Cress and Mandarin Oil with a chilled glass of either the 2003 Kumeu River Chardonnay or the 2005 Kumeu River Maté's Vineyard Chardonnay. The former shows a lovely bottle-aged character and a particularly mineral note which cuts the richness of the crayfish, while the latter is younger and shows fresher fruit characters.

To discover Kumeu River's wines within the stylish ambience of The French Café is to synthesise three of New Zealand's key assets: its wine, its food and its people. Relax and enjoy this quintessentially Kiwi dining experience.

Kumeu River Wines

PRODUCTS
Chardonnay • Pinot Gris • Pinot Noir • Merlot • Sauvignon

FEATURES
cellar door tastings • winery tours by appointment

NEARBY
Muriwai Beach • BeesOnline Honey Centre & Café • golf • mountain biking

CONTACT
550 State Highway 16, PO Box 24, Kumeu 0841 •
telephone: +64.9.412 8415 •
facsimile: +64.9.412 7627 •
email: enquiries@kumeuriver.co.nz •
website: www.kumeuriver.co.nz

The French Café

SEATS
dining area: 80 • al fresco area: 20

FOOD
contemporary European

DRINK
Old World and New World wines

FEATURES
bar • conservatory room • courtyard

CONTACT
210 Symonds Street, Auckland 1010 •
telephone: +64.9.377 1911 •
website: www.thefrenchcafe.co.nz

lawson's dry hills +
herzog luxury restaurant

...intense flavour and expressive varietal characters.

Situated in Marlborough, the largest wine-making region in New Zealand, is a winery which has come a long way since its humble beginnings in 1992. Lawson's Dry Hills may have first started out from an old tin shed, but today it is recognised as one of the leading wine-producers in New Zealand. Founded by Ross and Barbara Lawson, the winery has successfully maintained its close family and team environment. Notably, Ross was also the founding president of the 'New Zealand Screwcap Wine Seal Initiative', with the aim of enhancing the quality of their wines.

Lawson's Dry Hills Gewürztraminer, which the wine-makers initially produced from their own small vineyard, was soon recognised as one of the country's finest. It was this achievement that raised the winery's status both nationally and internationally. Following the success of this rich and spicy white wine, subsequent plantings gave rise to what is now the vineyard's main highlight and favourite amongst wine-lovers: Sauvignon Blanc.

Owing to the prime location of the vineyards, Lawson's Dry Hills Winery offers high quality wine with attributes such as an intense flavour and expressive varietal characters. Lying east-west and enjoying a maritime climate, the Wairau River Valley maximises the wonderfully-long clear sunny days, especially evident during the autumn ripening period. These long days are balanced by cooler nights, lengthening the ripening process and in turn, intensifying the fruit flavours and subsequently the wine.

THIS PAGE (FROM ABOVE): The vineyards are covered with netting as an effective protection from birds; high ceilings accentuate the spaciousness of the restaurant.

OPPOSITE (FROM TOP): The entrance to Lawson's Dry Hills winery; the Marlborough Crayfish is a speciality popular with Herzog's diners.

Swirl a sip of Lawson's Dry Hills 2006 Sauvignon Blanc around the palate and experience the crisp acidity of passionfruit and lime. These flavours dominate the nose with quiet hints of barrel ferment. Concentrated gooseberry, lime zest and red pepper balance the weight of this wine, leaving a clean, brisk finish. These complex flavours are the result of harvesting grapes over a dozen vineyards and across a range of soil types—from light stony soils to heavy loam, including a relatively large proportion of clay-based soil.

Indeed, Lawson's Dry Hills has lived up to its aim of producing wines which reflect its distinct climate and environment. On its list, aside from the acclaimed Sauvignon Blanc and Gewürztraminer, are Lawson's Riesling, Chardonnay, Pinot Gris and Pinot Noir, all of which respectively exhibit the desired concentration and balance of flavours.

MARLBOROUGH CRAYFISH WITH LEMON CONFIT, BEURRE BLANC AND POTATO MASH
Serves 4

Crayfish
2 live crayfish, each about 400g (14 oz) • 2 tbsp olive oil • 1 garlic clove, crushed • 2 tbsp unsalted butter • Maldon sea salt and ground white pepper, to taste

Lemon confit
1 lemon, sliced thinly • 150 g (5 oz) rock salt • 100 ml (3 fl oz) olive oil

Beurre blanc
300 ml (10 fl oz) fish stock • 100 ml (3 fl oz) sparkling wine or white wine • 1 bay leaf • 50 g (2 oz) sour cream • 80 g (3 oz) unsalted butter • Maldon sea salt, pepper and Tabasco sauce, to taste • juice of ½ a lemon • 3 mint leaves

Potato mash
500 g (17 ½ oz) Agria potatoes • 1 garlic clove, crushed • 100 ml (3 fl oz) cream • 50 g (2 oz) butter • salt, pepper and nutmeg, to taste

Crayfish Boil the crayfish at least for 1 minute in water and cool it down with ice water. Cut it in 2 length-wise. Sear in pan with the olive oil, garlic and fresh unsalted butter for about 4 minutes.
Lemon confit Cover lemon slices with rock salt and leave refrigerated for 24 hours. Rinse the slices with water and dry on a paper towel. Place the slices in a little container and pour over the olive oil. Refrigerate before serving.
Beurre blanc Combine the stock with the wine and bay leaf in a saucepan and bring to a boil. Simmer the stock until reduced to almost ½ the quantity. Add sour cream and the butter and stir with a whisk until dissolved. Season with Maldon sea salt, pepper, Tabasco sauce and lemon juice. Chop the mint and 2 slices of the lemon confit into fine strips and add to the sauce. Use a bar mixer to create froth on the beurre blanc.
Potato mash Boil the potatoes with garlic in salt water until tender and mash with a potato press. Add cream, butter, and season with salt, pepper and nut meg to taste.
To serve Take the crayfish meat out of the shells and cut it in 2 pieces. Season with salt and pepper, top with lemon confit and a beurre blanc sauce, and serve with potato mash.

Lawson's wines have been listed on the menu of several renowned restaurants in New Zealand. One of them is Herzog Luxury Restaurant, voted 'best destination-dining experience in the country' by New Zealand's leading food writer, Lauraine Jacobs, for *Cuisine* magazine. With a cast of chefs originally from Michelin-starred restaurants in Europe, it is a mecca for gourmets who come here to sample market-fresh gourmet cuisine in a world-class ambience. A recommended pairing would be Lawson's Sauvignon Blanc and Marlborough Crayfish with Lemon Confit, Beurre Blanc and Potato Mash. The citrus taste of the dry white wine works well with the crayfish, heightening its flavour. The restaurant and bistro at Herzog estate opens for dinner and lunch from Tuesday to Sunday, from October to end of May.

Lawson's Dry Hills

PRODUCTS
Chardonnay • Gewürztraminer • Riesling • Pinot Gris • Pinot Noir • Pinot Rosé • Sauvignon Blanc

FEATURES
cellar door

NEARBY
Wither Hills

CONTACT
Alabama Road, PO Box 4020, Redwood Village, Blenheim 7242 • telephone: +64.3.578 7674 • facsimile: +64.3.578 7603 • email: wine@lawsonsdryhills.co.nz • website: www.lawsonsdryhills.co.nz

Herzog Luxury Restaurant

SEATS
restaurant: 60 • private dining room: 12 • cellar door bistro: 30 • gardens: 50 • winery for aperitif: 100

FOOD
modern European

DRINK
over 550 vintage labels inclusive of Herzog's single vineyard wines

FEATURES
winery • walk-in wine cellar • lounge • extensive cigar and digestive list

CONTACT
81 Jeffries Rd, RD 3, Blenheim 7273 • telephone: +64.3.572 8770 • facsimile: +64.3.572 8730 • email: info@herzog.co.nz • website: www.herzog.co.nz

the millton vineyard +
the wharf café, bar + restaurant

...balancing earth, water, air and light.

THIS PAGE *(CLOCKWISE FROM RIGHT)*: *The 2005 Clos de Ste. Anne complete range of wines; Millton's ebony bottle caps; these grapes have been organically grown without any chemical input.*

OPPOSITE *(FROM TOP)*: *Bees and lavender are a common sight around the winery; the harbourside location draws a steady stream of casual diners to The Wharf Café, Bar & Restaurant.*

Gisborne may be a popular seaside destination in New Zealand but today, with a successful wine-making industry, this region is also known as the 'Chardonnay Capital' of New Zealand.

Wine tours are enjoyable adjuncts to any visit to Gisborne, where travellers get to discover the idyllic coastline of the region and the 60-hectare (150-acre) Eastwoodhill Arboretum, which has the largest collection of Northern Hemisphere trees in the Southern Hemisphere.

In harmony with these tranquil and natural environs is The Millton Vineyard, based in Poverty Bay and located 5 km (3 miles) from the sea. Run by James and Annie Millton, the establishment was touted as the 'Most Exciting Wine Company' by the *National Business Review* in 2006.

Working in the French and German wine industries inspired the Milltons to head back to New Zealand and establish their own winery in 1984, on the banks of the Te Arai River. The first grapevines were planted here in 1871 by early settlers.

Since then, their wines have won accolades for various competitions, one of which is the International Organic Wine Challenge for the Chardonnay. Millton's Te Arai Chenin Blanc is in *Cuisine*'s Top 100, favoured for its vibrant fruitiness, sweetness and acidity. The Millton Vineyard brand also offers Malbec, Merlot and a delicious off-dry Riesling.

The Milltons' wine-growing is based on the principle of biodynamics. This method of organic agriculture follows Rudolf Steiner's theory of cosmic influence and balancing earth, water, air and light. Here, traditional viticulture is practised in all of The Millton's vineyards, reducing the need to rely on manufactured chemicals. The aim is for these agricultural activities is to leave the land in an improved condition for future generations to come. As wine writer Jancis Robinson once noted, 'James Millton started growing grapes biodynamically before it was even heard of in Burgundy'.

James, who has played a key role in the establishment of Certified Organic Winegrowers of New Zealand, and who was a prominent presenter at The First International Biodynamic Wine Forum in 2004, enjoys interacting with fellow wine-lovers at The Millton Vineyard. This leaves visitors assured of a down-to-earth wine-tasting session. The insightful tastings can be savoured in the winery's traditional English garden.

For a taste of Millton's wines by the harbour, visit The Wharf Café, Bar & Restaurant, which is a 15-minute drive from The Millton Vineyard. This city establishment has a timeless maritime appeal. Its Pacific Rim-inspired menu offers fresh produce from Gisborne and prides itself on serving local wines.

For the entrée, Chef Dave Oglias recommends the Fresh Seared Marinated Yellow Fin Tuna with Strawberry Salad and Wasabi Pure Orange Dressing. The meal is best paired with 2005 Millton Chenin Blanc. The wine's honeyed tones are freshened by hints of apple and pebbly notes, balancing out the savoury dish.

The Wharf's Angus Scotch Fillet of Beef with Zucchini Balls and Stilton Butter calls for something meatier. The 2005 Millton Clos de Ste. Anne Pinot Noir's ripe strawberry nose and fine-grained tannins will subtly complement the rich flavours of this dish. When it comes to dessert, the Essencia Chardonnay Individual Bunch Selection is highly recommended to take on the spicy-sweet Cardamom Crusted Crème Brulée.

So while in Gisborne's pristine surroundings, savour wine as nature intended with the organic and authentic wines of The Millton Vineyard.

The Millton Vineyard

PRODUCTS
Ranges: Clos de Ste. Anne,
The Millton Vineyard

FEATURES
cellar door tastings • wine sales

NEARBY
Eastwood Hill Arboretum • fly fishing •
water sports

CONTACT
CMB 66, Manutuke, Gisborne 4053 •
telephone: +64.6.862 8680 •
facsimile: +64.6.862 8869 •
email: inspired@millton.co.nz •
website: www.millton.co.nz

The Wharf Café, Bar + Restaurant

SEATS
dining area: 60 • al fresco area: 30

FOOD
contemporary Pacific Rim

DRINK
New Zealand, Australian and
Old World wine list

FEATURE
harbour view

CONTACT
60 The Esplanade, Gisborne 4010 •
telephone: +64.6.868 4876 •
facsimile: +64.6.868 4876
email: lew@wharfbar.co.nz •
website: www.wharfbar.co.nz

nautilus estate of marlborough +
antoine's restaurant

The cellar design takes its inspiration from the geometric curves of the Nautilus shell...

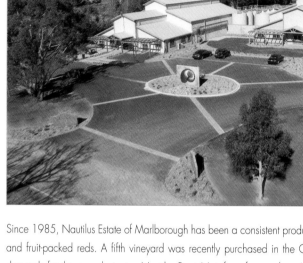

THIS PAGE (CLOCKWISE FROM RIGHT): An aerial view of the expansive winery grounds; the Sauvignon Blanc is most noticeable for its crisp acidity; a conducive terroir facilitates the growth of Nautilus' vines.

OPPOSITE (FROM TOP): Italian Sushi with Smoked Salmon, Bell Peppers and Zucchini, served on a chilled saffron consommé with salmon caviar; the restaurant's interior design follows a modern New York theme.

Since 1985, Nautilus Estate of Marlborough has been a consistent producer of flawless whites and fruit-packed reds. A fifth vineyard was recently purchased in the Omaka Valley to meet demands for the award-winning Nautilus Pinot Noir from fans such as London's Le Pont de la Tour restaurant and New York's The Waldorf-Astoria.

The winery's colour scheme reflects its local environment. Its gravelly tones and natural timbers create a distinctly contemporary feel. The cellar design takes its inspiration from the geometric curves of the Nautilus shell logo. Its underground wine library provides optimum storage conditions. The modern cellar door is the first port of call for many, with well-organised tours and friendly staff offering tempting cheese platters, a sensory testing station and advice on wine-tasting techniques.

In 2000, Nautilus opened the Southern Hemisphere's first cellar dedicated solely to producing the mouth-watering Pinot Noir. The state-of-the-art white winery, completed just hours before the arrival of its first grapes in 2006, provides the ultimate starting point for a tour of Marlborough's greatest wine-producers.

Wine-maker Clive Jones recommends the winery's Sauvignon Blanc, awarded 'Best Sauvignon Blanc in the World' at the International Wine Challenge in 1995. It boasts Marlborough's typical aroma of melon, lime, gooseberry and passion fruit, with red pepper and nettle on a mid-weight palate. Its Gold Medal-winning qualities are evident from the first appealing sip.

Nautilus deems Antoine's Restaurant in Auckland to be the ideal and most conducive environment in which to savour its wines. Clive Jones and restaurateur Tony Astle both share a life-long passion for their respective crafts, making this a natural pairing.

This benchmark Auckland establishment was set up in 1973 and has a guest list as

glittering as Nautilus' awards. The elegant interior is stately and traditional and the service relaxed but immaculate. Providing silver service without the pomp, it appeals to a wide age range. The dishes are presented creatively and boast a great diversity of flavours. Its wine list spirals from its core emphasis on local wines out to great wines from around the world.

The main course, Ox Tongue Simmered in Madeira and Green Peppercorns, is best savoured with a glass of Nautilus Pinot Noir, which brings out a whiff of plums and dark fruits. The Tuna Trio (thinly sliced as carpaccio, chopped as tartare and seared and tucked inside a spring roll) requires the lighter touch of a chilled Nautilus Estate Sauvignon Blanc. Antoine's 'Nostalgic Menu' features dishes still popular today, such as Traditional Roast Duckling with Orange and Grand Marnier Sauce. Make the dining experience more memorable with a gently effervescent glass of Nautilus Marlborough Brut NV.

As winery owner Robert Hill Smith says, 'We don't want to make 'nice' wines. We want to make great wines, wines of distinction'. Taste them in person at Antoine's, Auckland's longest-running fine dining restaurant.

Nautilus Estate of Marlborough

PRODUCTS
Cuvée Marlborough Brut NV • Pinot Noir 2005 • Sauvignon Blanc 2006 • Chardonnay 2004 • Pinot Gris 2006

FEATURES
Wine Room and Interpretive Centre • wine-tasting

NEARBY
scenic flights • golf • fishing • dolphin watching

CONTACT
12 Rapaura Road, Renwick, Marlborough 7243 •
telephone: +64.3.572 9364 •
facsimile: +64.3.572 9374 •
email: sales@nautilusestate.com •
website: www.nautilusestate.com

Antoine's Restaurant

SEATS
main dining area: 50 • courtyard: 20

FOOD
New Zealand and French

DRINK
Old World and New World wines

FEATURE
courtyard

CONTACT
333 Parnell Road, PO Box 37395, Parnell, Auckland 1001 •
telephone: +64.9.379 8756 •
facsimile: +64.9.524 0684 •
email: antoines@xtra.co.nz •
website: www.antoinesrestaurant.co.nz/restaurant.html

neudorf vineyards +
hopgood's restaurant + bar

...growing great grapes and making great wine.

Established in 1978 by Tim and Judy Finn, Neudorf Vineyards sits in the Moutere Hills in Nelson, at the top of South Island. The region's climate is well-suited to aromatic varieties, with Neudorf Sauvignon Blanc, Pinot Gris and Riesling sought after for their elegance and texture.

A visit to Neudorf offers not just a chance to taste some of the area's finest wines but also a valuable lesson in terroir. Tim attributes the unique quality of Neudorf's wines to the combination of ancient clay-gravel soils, long, gentle summers and cool, autumn nights.

At Neudorf, wines are treasured for their sense of place. Their two vineyard sites produce wines which vary distinctly from each other. The free-draining alluvial soils at Brightwater produce wines with tight, bright aromatics, while the clay-gravel hillsides of the Moutere encourage texture and complexity. As one noted wine critic said, 'When you want lucidity and rhythm in a wine, then Neudorf is your vineyard.'

Always looking for purity and poise, life at Neudorf is structured around pushing the boundaries. The Finns have found it immensely satisfying to be growing grapes and making wine from such terroir, and being able to witness the combination of quality factors change with a vintage and evolve with the age of the vines.

Neudorf Moutere Chardonnay, widely regarded as one of New Zealand's finest, has a seemingly permanent place on the wine lists of a number of London's Michelin-starred restaurants. Only 500 cases are produced each year, and these are usually spoken for within

THIS PAGE (CLOCKWISE FROM ABOVE):
Mud-brick was used to construct Neudorf's wine cellar; scarlet red borders stand out against the greenery.
OPPOSITE (FROM TOP): Neudorf's main entrance is marked by a German-style signboard; wooden floors and ambient lighting complement the warm interiors of Hopgood's; the restaurant's elegant entrance is one of several which line Trafalgar Street, Nelson's shopping and central business district.

a fortnight of their September release. Neudorf's Moutere Pinot Noir is also up there with the best—a gloriously seductive wine with finely textured tannins wrapped around a core of ripe fruit, giving way to an attenuated finish of juicy minerality.

Neudorf has a portfolio of knowledgeable wine distributors who handle their markets in the UK, Europe and the US. Tim notes that the business is lucky to have these dedicated oenophiles on board, for they allow the team at Neudorf to put their energies into what they do best—growing great grapes and making great wine.

Food enthusiasts who wish to sample Neudorf's wines with authentic Nelson cuisine should have a meal at Hopgood's Restaurant & Bar, located on Trafalgar Street in Nelson's central business district. Owner and Chef Kevin Hopgood, who has worked alongside culinary greats such as Gordon Ramsay and the Roux brothers, serves a carefully selected menu of dishes using the best seasonal ingredients that Nelson has to offer.

Chef Hopgood cites the pairing of his Chicken Liver Parfait with Walnut and Raisin Toast with Neudorf's Moutere Chardonnay as a combination that leaves the palate sparkling with excitement. And to accompany Neudorf's Moutere Pinot Noir, his seasonal offering of Assiette of Lamb with Fondant Potato, Confit Garlic and Black Olive Jus is an ideal match. These pairings culminate in a gastronomic experience found only in the heart of Nelson.

Neudorf Vineyards

PRODUCTS
Chardonnay • Sauvignon Blanc • Riesling • Pinot Gris • Pinot Noir • Rosé • Verjuice

FEATURES
cellar door • wine-tasting

NEARBY
horse treks • shopping • arts and crafts

CONTACT
Neudorf Road, Upper Moutere, Nelson 7175 • telephone: +64.3.543 2643 • facsimile: +64.3.543 2955 • email: wine@neudorf.co.nz • website: www.neudorf.co.nz

Hopgood's Restaurant + Bar

SEATS
dining area: 40 • al fresco area: 20

FOOD
contemporary French

DRINK
Nelson beers • New Zealand premier wines

CONTACT
284 Trafalgar Street, Nelson 7010 • telephone: +64.3.545 7191 • fascimile: +64.3.545 7151 email: hopgoods@xtra.co.nz

palliser estate wines of martinborough + boulcott street bistro

...wines of great complexity and character.

THIS PAGE (CLOCKWISE FROM ABOVE):
At a latitude of 40 degrees south, the vineyard's location is ideal for growing wine; lush greenery fills the winery's front surrounds; a distinct citrus flavour and acidity dominates this wine.

OPPOSITE (FROM TOP): *Boulcott Street Bistro's Fillet Béarnaise with Pomme Frites; the bistro's main dining area; Victorian architecture is evident from the bistro's façade.*

In the Wairarapa region, at the foot of the North Island, lies a scenic river valley known as Martinborough. Situated to the east of the Tararua Ranges and Rimutaka Hill, this is a quaint destination with myriad restaurants and heritage sites located within walking distance.

Popular with aficionados of New Zealand wine, Martinborough houses many top boutique wineries and premium Pinot Noir producers. Allan Johnson is the chief wine-maker at one of the most impressive wineries, Palliser Estate Wines of Martinborough. In the Burgundy-like climate of this wine-grower's paradise, Allan's driving ambition is to create 'delicious varietal wines that reflect the best of Martinborough'.

The winery is accommodated in modern buildings reminiscent of old stables bordering a sheltered courtyard, creating a pleasant, quiet place to have a picnic and to enjoy wine-tasting. With its first vineyards planted in 1984, Palliser maintains 69 hectares (173 acres) of vines in the renowned Martinborough Terraces.

The Estate produces two ranges of wines. The Palliser Estate label, which represents their premium range, includes Riesling, Pinot Gris, Sauvignon Blanc, Chardonnay, Pinot Noir and a sparkling wine, Methode Traditionnelle. Pencarrow is Palliser's second-tier brand and comprises Sauvignon Blanc, Chardonnay and Pinot Noir.

The Palliser Estate Pinot Noir is featured on exclusive wine lists worldwide and served on some of the leading global airlines. Palliser Estate wines are exported to 23 different countries, and since 1989, have received an impressive list of trophies across all varietals.

An intimate atmosphere in which to enjoy Palliser's hand-crafted wines is that of Boulcott Street Bistro. Now a Wellington icon, the restaurant is located in a traditional Victorian house which was built in 1876. Its classic dishes are served with a modern edge and its diverse wine list supports many boutique wineries including leaders in their field, such as Palliser Estate wines.

Chef and co-owner Chris Green displays culinary skills which ensure that this contemporary bistro appeals to Wellinton's regular and most discerning visitors. His inviting starters include Grilled Asparagus with Crispy Pancetta, Mozzarella and Tomato Concassé.

A perfect complement to Chris Green's Fillet Béarnaise with Pomme Frites is Palliser Estate's Pinot Noir 2005. Its intense flavours and smooth tannins coupled with concentrated dark berry fruits enhance a soft lingering finish to match the classic French sauce of this dish.

Independent travellers seeking a wine and gastronomic experience should look no further than Boulcott Street Bistro.

Palliser Estate Wines of Martinborough

PRODUCTS
Palliser Estate range: Riesling, Pinot Gris, Sauvignon Blanc, Chardonnay, Pinot Noir, Methode Traditionnelle • Pencarrow range: Sauvignon Blanc, Chardonnay, Pinot Noir

FEATURES
cellar door • wine-tasting

NEARBY
The Martinborough Hotel • Brackenridge Country Retreat • Parehua Country Estate • Martinborough Wine Centre

CONTACT
Palliser Winery, PO Box 121, Kitchener St, Martinborough 5741 • telephone: +64.6.306 9019 • facsimile: +64.6.306 9946 • email: palliser@palliser.co.nz • website: www.palliser.co.nz

Boulcott Street Bistro

SEATS
main dining area: 45 • private dining room: 16

FOOD
contemporary international

DRINK
wine list • cellar list

CONTACT
99 Boulcott Street, Wellington 6011 • telephone: +64.4.499 4199 • facsimile: +64.4.499 3879 • email: info@boulcottstbistro.co.nz • website: www.boulcottstreetbistro.co.nz

pegasus bay winery + pescatore restaurant

...a haven for enthusiasts of fine wine, art and cuisine.

If staying in Christchurch on South Island's eastern coast, a leisurely day-trip to Canterbury should be inked into the itinerary of any self-respecting wine lover. From the adrenalin of jet-boating to the serenity of horse riding through neat farmlands and beech forests, Canterbury and its environs present plentiful opportunities for adventure. But when the real quest is to discover perfection in a bottle, a visit to Pegasus Bay Winery should take precedence.

Situated in the heart of the resplendent Waipara Valley, just 30 minutes north of the city, Pegasus Bay Winery is a haven for enthusiasts of fine wine, art and cuisine. Its informative tours, prestigious wines and restaurant conspire to create a pleasurable visit.

Oenological passions will be ignited in the atmospheric barrel hall and cellar beneath the winery. Avid fans of food and art are equally well catered for in the winery's own garden-view restaurant. The fresh flavours of its Kiwi-inspired dishes are complemented by the contemporary artworks of leading New Zealand artists, which are displayed on the wall. In an elegant yet casual setting, serious food is matched with serious wines produced by the estate.

Wine-writer, wine-judge and Professor of Neurology, Ivan Donaldson, along with his family, were pioneers of the region. They have been seriously involved in wine since the early 1970s and went on to plant the Pegasus Bay vineyard in 1985. Although it is their policy not to enter wine shows, many of their wines regularly receive five-star reviews in international publications such as *Decanter*, *Wine Spectator* and *Wine Enthusiast*.

As the region's leading producer of fine wines, Pegasus Bay exudes a certain 'je ne sais quoi', which appears effortless. Advocates of minimal intervention and traditional viticulture, the Donaldsons produce exquisitely-crafted and classic expressions of each varietal.

THIS PAGE (CLOCKWISE FROM ABOVE):
This row of vines adds a charming touch to the winery's exterior; the tasting room provides ample space for large groups.
OPPOSITE (FROM TOP): The Duo of New Zealand Lamb is a treat for the senses; Pescatore offers diners a view of Hagley Park; the chandeliers in Pegasus Bay's restaurant are impressive works of art.

Their range includes a multi-layered Pinot Noir which often shows a rare combination of power and finesse. Riesling is their key white varietal which is made in a luscious off-dry style, perfectly balanced by its knife-edge acidity. An avid fan of this wine is celebrated wine-writer Jancis Robinson. Pegasus Bay's traditional blend of Sauvignon Blanc and Semillon has many fans, due to its impressive mix of exotic fruits, complexity and texture. A range of reserve wines—Aria, Prima Donna, Maestro, Finale and Encore—was also produced in small quantities, and so named because of Ivan's wife Christine's love for opera.

Back in Christchurch, diners are encouraged to appreciate Pegasus Bay wines in the prestigious restaurant, Pescatore. It is sleekly located in The George Hotel, one of the best places to stay in the world, according to the *Condé Nast Traveler* Gold List 2007.

Pescatore's reputation as South Island's definitive dining destination is enhanced by its exemplary wine list. It features, among others, wines from Pegasus Bay's Waipara vineyard, such as the Chardonnay 2003.

The principal dish in Pescatore's six-course dégustation menu is its Duo of New Zealand Lamb served with Fondant Potato and Porcini Jus. Marry this meal with a Pegasus Bay Pinot Noir 2004 and let the fruity flavours intermingle with the caramelised mirepoix in the Porcini Jus. Set in an award-winning hotel restaurant, this pairing will leave even the toughest gourmet immensely satisfied.

Pegasus Bay Winery

PRODUCTS
Riesling • Sauvignon Semillon • Chardonnay • Pinot Noir • Merlot Cabernet • Aria Late Picked Riesling • Prima Donna Pinot Noir • Maestro Merlot Malbec • Finale Noble Chardonnay • Encore Noble Riesling

FEATURES
wine cellars • wine tours

NEARBY
jet-boating • horse riding • hunting • fishing

CONTACT
263 Stockgrove Road, RD 2, Amberley 7482, North Canterbury • telephone: +64.3.314 6869 • facsimile: +64.3.314 6861 • email: info@pegasusbay.com • website: www.pegasusbay.com

Pescatore Restaurant

SEATS
main dining area: 50 • private dining room: 12

FOOD
Pacific Rim

DRINK
local and international wine lists

FEATURE
garden view

CONTACT
The George Hotel, 50 Park Terrace, Canterbury 8001 • telephone: +64.3.371 0257 • facsimile: +64.3.366 6747 • email: fandb@thegeorge.com • website: www.thegeorge.com

villa maria estate + cibo restaurant

...home of New Zealand's most awarded wines.

THIS PAGE: *A wholesome experience beckons at the contemporary Auckland Winery and Vineyard Park.*

OPPOSITE (FROM TOP): *Villa Maria's Seddon Pinot Gris is best matched with Cibo's Three Little Asian Salads, a feast for the eyes as well as the palate; architecturally designed, the Marlborough Winery blends seamlessly into the surrounding landscape.*

Villa Maria Estate's new Auckland Winery and Vineyard Park is an all-inclusive treat for wine lovers. Designed by renowned architect Hamish Cameron, it was relocated in 2005 from the original winery site and recreated with the passion epitomising Villa Maria wines.

The complex is the brainchild of owner George Fistonich. In 1961, he founded Villa Maria, now home of New Zealand's most awarded wines. With a functional yet visually sleek design incorporating conference and entertainment facilities, the building reflects his vision to associate wine with other cultural experiences. A highlight is the viewing platform, beneath which the panorama of Puketutu Island, Manukau Harbour and central Auckland extends.

Located at the base of an extinct volcano, the gradient of the land provides Villa Maria with a natural amphitheatre, perfect for outdoor events such as The Auckland Philharmonia Orchestra's Summer Matinée. The mineral-rich soils in this area are also home to Chardonnay, Gewürztraminer and Verdelho vines. Following an informative tour of the winery, visitors can experience a tailor-made tasting of various trophy wines at the Cellar Door.

For the ultimate consistency in wine quality, every bottle is sealed with a screwcap instead of the conventional cork closure. The focus on technologically advanced methods to maintain the quality of its products has contributed to Villa Maria's success as New Zealand's leading wine award winner since the early 1980s.

The Estate also opened a Marlborough Winery in 2000, owing to the rapid growth of grape harvest in this premium grape-growing region, and for greater long-term expansion spanning the next five decades.

Villa Maria's four distinct ranges of wine exude finesse from prime vineyards in Marlborough, Hawkes Bay, Gisborne and Auckland. The extensive Private Bin range offers everyday, food-friendly wines; the Cellar

Selection wines are ripe, engaging and designed for immediate enjoyment or mid-term cellaring; the Reserve range boasts pure, more intense flavours; and the winery's pièce de résistance, the Single Vineyard range, is a limited-edition collection of benchmark excellence.

The best way to experience the wines of Villa Maria is through one of Auckland's best-kept secrets, Cibo. Since 1994, the restaurant has provided one of the city's finest wedding venues and great gastronomic indulgences. Situated in an old chocolate factory, the establishment was a finalist in *Cuisine* magazine's Restaurant of the Year Award 2006.

Chef Kate Fay's talent ensures a gratifying feast, while the staff maintains a professional yet casual atmosphere. Cibo dresses to impress with its striking interior, exotic fish pond and covered courtyard for stylish summer dining, and its wine list as an excellent accessory.

Savouring Chef Fay's Three Little Asian Salads alone is incomplete without Villa Maria's Seddon Pinot Gris. Intense on the palate, the wine's alluring pear-drop and spicy cinnamon aromas complement the fragile flavours of this delicate platter.

For a fresh and fruity dessert, pair Villa Maria's Reserve Noble Riesling with Cibo's signature melt-in-the-mouth Raspberry and Strawberry Sorbet Shortcake. The tartness of this dish is perfectly balanced with the sweetness of the Noble Riesling, which has a lingering finish.

Villa Maria Auckland Winery and Vineyard Park

WINES
Private Bin • Cellar Selection • Reserve • Single Vineyard

FEATURES
entertainment venues • viewing platform • a Master of Wine • wine-tasting • winery tours

BUSINESS
conference facilities

NEARBY
Auckland International Airport • Otuataua Stonefields • Puketutu Island

CONTACTS
Villa Maria Auckland Winery, 118 Montgomerie Rd, PO Box 43046, Mangere, Auckland • telephone: +64.9.255 0660 • facsimile: +64.9.255 0661 • email: enquiries@villamaria.co.nz • website: www.villamaria.co.nz

Cibo Restaurant

SEATS
dining area: 80 • al fresco area: 120

FOOD
New Zealand and international

DRINK
Old and New World wines

FEATURES
private courtyard • garden view

CONTACT
91 St Georges Bay Road, PO Box 37234, Parnell, Auckland • telephone: +64.9.303 9660 • facsimile: +64.9.303 9661 • email: enquiry@cibo.co.nz • website: www.cibo.co.nz

antipodes water +
white restaurant at hilton auckland

...exclusively produced for restaurant dining.

New Zealand's water has long been renowned for its purity. Indeed, this is part of the country's heritage and is best embodied in Antipodes Water. The brainchild of founder Simon Woolley, Antipodes was created to meet the growing demand for softly-beaded mineral water which is exclusively produced for restaurant dining.

A big water drinker himself, Woolley, who was also a restaurateur, often wondered why he had to import water from Europe, when better artesian water should instead be sourced from his homeland. He spent two years researching on the composition of New Zealand waters, and the result is the deepest, highest quality groundwater in the country, encased in a bottle that is as pure and simple as its contents.

Antipodes' water is sourced from a deep aquifer of about 150 to 300 m (492 to 984 ft) below ground level. At this depth, pressure ensures that any seepage is outward rather than inward, which eliminates contamination and keeps the water pure. It is then drawn to the surface and bottled at source in Whakatane, Bay of Plenty.

Antipodes was created solely for top restaurants, lodges, hotels and caterers, so these bottles will not be found on the shelves of supermarkets or the local bottle store. The water's pure taste never distracts from the flavours of the food, which explains why 34 out of New Zealand's 40 best restaurants make Antipodes their table water of choice.

One such establishment is White Restaurant, named 'Restaurant of The Year' at New Zealand's Culinary Fare in 2004. Housed in the five-star Hilton Auckland at the end of Princes Wharf, it is surrounded by the gleaming waters of Waitemata Harbour. As its name suggests, this whitewashed restaurant is like a blank canvas, where the ever-changing reflection of light from the surrounding waters casts a different glow depending on the weather and time of day.

From shimmering shades of blues to deep greens, the reflection of light plays against the restaurant's floor-to-ceiling windows, which offers panoramic views across the harbour. Patrons sit on white leather chairs, set upon white marble floors. The crisp table linen and fine Rosenthal china are all white too.

The restaurant's impeccable dishes are created by Executive Chef, Bernard Bernabe.

THIS PAGE (CLOCKWISE FROM ABOVE): Exclusively produced for fine dining and home delivery, Antipodes' water is bottled in a clean and simple design; the sparkling water offers the softest bead to enhance digestion.

OPPOSITE (CLOCKWISE FROM TOP): The Chef's Tasting of Ice Creams and Sorbet served on Tuille and Trio of Coulis; the interior of White was created by Dan Kwan of Tribeca, a design firm based in Singapore; diners can enjoy clear views of the harbour while feasting indoors.

His is a seasonal menu which is always a blend of harmonised flavours and textures inspired by New Zealand's finest products and the latest international culinary trends. Chef Bernabe likes to call it 'a celebration of the palate'.

The fitting way to sample Bernabe's exquisite works is to order the dégustation menu, in which each dish is paired with a wine. His appetisers include a robust Crayfish Bisque Crème with Dill Mascarpone, and Seared Scallops served with Minted Pea Purée, Trio of Basil, White Speck, and Lime Butter Sauce. After a palate cleanser of Champagne Granita and Campari Jelly comes the main event—Chargrilled Beef Fillet, Kumara Rosti, Sautéed Kale, Mushrooms and Beef Consommé. To end this delectable feast on a sweet note, try the New Zealand dessert special, Kapiti Brick with Pickled Cherries and Brioche Croute, or a Valrhona Chocolate Fondant with Vanilla Anglaise and Macerated Cherries.

Antipodes Water

PRODUCTS
sparkling and still artesian table water

FEATURES
bottled at source • worldwide distribution • home and office delivery

CONTACT
421 St Lukes, PO Box 41, Auckland 1346 • telephone: +64.9.846 9651 • facsimile: +64.9.846 9650 • email: info@antipodes.co.nz • website: www.antipodes.co.nz

White Restaurant at Hilton Auckland

SEATS
dining area: 80 • outdoor terrace: 30 • The Boardroom: 12

FOOD
international

DRINK
extensive wine list

FEATURES
harbour view • Tribeca design

CONTACT
Prince Wharf, 147 Quay Street, Auckland 1010 • telephone: +64.9.978 2020 • facsimile: +64.9.978 2001 • email: team@whiterestaurant.co.nz • website:www.whiterestaurant.co.nz

air new zealand

...long-haul travel never looked this good.

THIS PAGE (CLOCKWISE FROM RIGHT):
With a comfortable 180-degree lie-flat bed, passengers can enjoy a peaceful slumber; enjoy true fine dining in the Business Premier Class cabin; the menu gives passengers a genuine taste of New Zealand.

OPPOSITE (CLOCKWISE FROM TOP):
Air New Zealand features state-of-the-art passenger aircraft, ensuring long-haul travel in style and comfort; the in-flight skincare products are made with a blend of eco-friendly and native ingredients; privacy and convenience go hand-in-hand with the new herringbone seat layout in the Business Premier Class.

As an airline that flies some of the world's longest routes, Air New Zealand certainly knows how to provide in-flight comfort. With daily services to New Zealand via Los Angeles and Hong Kong, customers can enjoy the relaxed sense of calm they experience with Air New Zealand, which is the only true round-the-world single airline service from the UK.

Its Business Premier Class cabin features first-class amenities and service. Leather armchairs convert into 180-degree lie-flat beds, while large, adjustable tables allow passengers to dine together as if they were in a restaurant. This is made possible by an Ottoman footrest which doubles as a visitor's seat. A unique herringbone seat layout also allows passengers to have direct access to the aisles. If they prefer to lounge in their seats, however, a 26.4-cm (10.4-in) high-resolution entertainment screen and a noise-cancellation headset allow passengers to enjoy on-demand movies and music, the very latest in entertainment. Indeed, long-haul travel never looked this good.

Business travel is made easier with in-seat power for portable electronic devices such as laptops. A retractable cocktail tray and water bottle-holder ensure that passengers can keep well-hydrated throughout the flight. Business Premier customers can take advantage of a complimentary chauffeur service up to 89 km (55 miles) from London Heathrow, leaving the stress of driving through the traffic, to someone else. Passengers can also make their own journey to London Heathrow smoother with a complimentary 30-day valet parking service.

Pacific Premium Economy is an exclusive class of travel which sits comfortably between Business Premier and Pacific Economy, with extra leg-room and exclusive cabin space. Passengers can enjoy more space than Pacific Economy with a seat pitch of 96.5 cm to 101.6 cm (38 in to 40 in), providing extra leg room to stretch out. Passengers may access

premium check-in counters at the airport and enjoy premium meals and finest New Zealand wine selections. The stellar team of Air New Zealand's consultant chefs includes Kiwi Peter Gordon, who is the chef behind the range at The Providores and Tapa Room in London, and Geoff Scott, the owner of famed New Zealand restaurant, Vinnies. The latest culinary trends are introduced through their award-winning cuisine.

The Pacific Premium Economy Class also offers Air New Zealand amenity kits which feature one of the country's largest skincare and make-up brands, Living Nature. This company strongly promotes its New Zealand heritage through harnessing the proven science of the natural healing and hydrating properties of native plants such as Manuka, Harekeke (flax), Kawakawa, Kumerahou, and kelp, often gathered in the wild from remote locations. Its organic products are just what travellers need to revitalise themselves during their long flights.

With all that it has to offer, the world-class airline leaves globe-trotters coming back for more travel opportunities to and from beautiful New Zealand itself.

DESTINATIONS
London • New Zealand • Los Angeles • Hong Kong

IN-FLIGHT
Business Premier Class: 180-degree lie-flat leather beds, direct aisle access for each seat, Ottoman visitor's seat, on-demand audio and video • Pacific Premium Economy Class: premium food and wine • Pacific Economy Class: on-demand audio and video

GROUND
Business Premier Class: complimentary chauffeur service, complimentary valet parking service for up to 30 days (both services applicable only in the UK) • Pacific Premium Economy Class: Business Premier check-in service

CONTACT
book online: www.airnewzealand.co.uk • UK reservations: 0800 028 4149 (24 hrs)

new zealand itineraries

New Zealand offers a plethora of activities, alluring travellers with diverse tastes in leisure and luxury. The real challenge lies in knowing where to even begin discovering the best Kiwi experiences and travel options. While the itineraries listed here encompass many of the properties profiled in this publication, customised ones may also be arranged.

Suggested itineraries

- Meet the Locals:

  New Zealand is not only rich in history but in culture too, especially that of the Maori community. Authentic local experiences are brought to life by expert guides who will help unlock the past and provide a personal insight into the way real Kiwis live today. From indigenous Maori food trails deep in native bush to private viewings of distinctive local artists at work, discover the essence of living in New Zealand.

  (Suggested duration: 10 days, November to March)

- Nature's Best:

  Enjoy New Zealand's scenery and wildlife encounters from the comfort and convenience of a private helicopter—a highly recommended mode of transport for this tour. Soar through the sky, and witness the sheer remoteness of some otherwise inaccessible landscapes.Get up close and personal with the native wildlife in an entirely safe and natural environment. See it all, from live volcanoes to towering fiords and from wild dolphins to pristine forests.

  (Suggested duration: 15 days, from November to March)

- **Pure Indulgence:**

  Six of New Zealand's world-famous, award-winning lodges and boutique hotels are selected to suit one's needs in this pleasurable two-week tour. Indulge in personal spa treatments or engage in a wide range of activities such as heli-fishing, golf, trekking and mountain biking. The list goes on, and is limited only by one's imagination.

  (Suggested duration: 10 days, from November to March)

- **Fresh Tracks:**

  Select the ultimate heli-skiing or snowboarding experience in the Southern Alps of New Zealand. The terrain spans vast areas of virgin powder without the typical large ski resorts dominating the horizon. This is wilderness skiing at its best, with spectacular views thrown in for good measure. Leave the crowds behind and head for the backcountry with a professional ski guide and specialist heli-ski operators for the ride of your life. Luxurious accommodation is provided, and so are helicopter transfers to and from all areas.

  (Suggested duration: 8 days, from July to September)

- **New World Wines:**

  Visit some of the top family-run New Zealand vineyards from the award-winning Family of Twelve wineries. In just two short decades, New Zealand wines have grown from relative obscurity to achieving an envied international reputation of producing some of the best wines in the world. The main focus may be on Sauvignon Blanc and Chardonnay, but notable awards have also been achieved by both Pinot Noir and Champagne. Tours to leading wineries are combined with lush boutique accommodation and the distinctive Pacific Rim cuisine. Travel by private car or by aircraft, depending on the schedule.

  (Suggested duration: 10 days, from November to March)

THIS PAGE (FROM ABOVE): The alpine landscapes offer thrilling powder descents for heli-skiers; food and wine form an integral part of the local lifestyle.

OPPOSITE (FROM TOP LEFT): Visitors will come to appreciate the essence of Maori culture with its enchanting performing arts; learn about New Zealand's lush native foliage through insightful forest walks; glacier landings allow travellers to get closer to nature.

NEW W◉RLD SAFARIS

Discover our world, your way

New World Safaris is a 100-per cent New Zealand-owned and operated luxury travel advisor which specialises in ready-made or customised itineraries for the ultimate Kiwi holiday. With the advantages of 24-hour support and the latest updates on New Zealand's unique range of accommodation, they advise travellers on the best *New Zealand Chic* properties that best suit their personal preference. To plan a holiday with ease, contact New World Safaris via email at nzchic@newworldsafaris.com, Skype: nzluxury, phone on +64.7.572 2233, or visit their website at www.newworldsafaris.com.

index

index

The publisher would like to thank the following for permission to reproduce their photographs:

Accolades Boutique Hotel back cover (below left), 74–75
Aflo Foto Agency/Photolibrary 130
Air New Zealand 216–217
Altrendo Travel/Getty 12
Andy Belcher/Photolibrary 50
Andy Whale/Getty 4
Anthony Blake/Photolibrary 174
Anthony Cassidy/Photolibrary 112
Antipodes Water 214
Antoine's Restaurant 205
Ata Rangi 190, 191 (top)
Baerbel Schmidt/Getty 6
Blanket Bay 138–139
The Boatshed front cover (below centre), 43 (below), 76–77
Boulcott Street Bistro 209
The Bridgeman Art Library/Getty 15 (below)
Browns Sotheby's International Realty 166–167
Cardrona Terrace Estate 140–141
Carl Warner/Getty 51 (top)
The Castle Matakana back cover (below right), 78–79
Chad Ehlers/Getty 41
Cibo Restaurant 213 (top)
Claremont Country Estate 142–143
Clearwater Cruises 108 (both on left), 109 (both below)
Colin Monteath/Photolibrary 135
Corina Lecca 43 (top)
Corinne Humphrey/Photolibrary 29
Craggy Range Winery 192
Dana Edmunds/Photolibrary 17 (below),
Dave Houser/Photolibrary 21 (top),
David Fleetham/Photolibrary 33 (below right)
David Kallick 120 (below)
David Wall/Getty 25 (top), 123
Delamore Lodge 80–81
Derek Henderson front cover (clothes), 42
Doug Armand/Getty 46

Doug Pearson/Photolibrary 132
Douglas Pearson/Corbis 40
Eichardt's Private Hotel 144–145
The Family of Twelve 188–189
Felix Oppenheim/Photolibrary 61
Felton Road 194, 195 (below right)
FoodPix/Photolibrary 116 (below)
Frans Lantin/Corbis 110
The French Café 199 (below)
Fromm Winery La Strada 196, 197 (top)
George Steinmetz/Corbis 14
Gerald Lopez 47
Gerard Soury/Photolibrary 115 (below)
Gibb's Vineyard Restaurant 197 (both on right; below)
Glacier Southern Lakes Helicopters 172–173
GmbH & Co KG/Photolibrary 185
Hapuku Lodge front flap (top), 146–147
HELiPRO 108 (top), 109 (top)
Heritage Hotel + Spa du Vin 82–83
Herzog Luxury Restaurant 200 (below), 201 (left)
Hopgood's Restaurant + Bar 207 (centre; below right)
Hotel Off The Square front flap (middle), 148–149
Huka Lodge front flap (below), 84–85
Huntley House 150–151
Japack Photo Library/Photolibrary 27 (right)
Jason Hosking/Photolibrary front cover (starfish), 38
Jeremy Walker/Getty 72
Jochen Schienker/Getty 136
John Banagan/Getty 127
JTB Photo/Photolibrary 121, 122 (top)
Ken Gillham/Photolibrary 56
Kevin Fleming/Corbis 134 (below)
Kevin Judd/Photolibrary front cover (vineyard), 62, 176
Kieran Scott/Photolibrary 36 (top right)
Kim Westerskov/Getty 53
Kincaid Lodge 152–153
Kumeu River Wines 198, 199 (top)
Kyle George/Getty 33 (top)

Lawson's Dry Hills 200 (top), 201 (top)
Lloyd Park 131 (top), 133 (below), 134 (top)
Lodge at 199 86–87
The Lodge at Paratiho Farms 154–155
Lorraine Shaw/Getty 179 (top)
Loungepark/Getty 2
Luca Trovato/Getty back cover (vineyard meal), 178
Martin Ruegner/Getty 186
Matakauri Lodge 156–157
Michael DeYoung/Photolibrary 59
Michael Le Poer Trench/Corbis 23 (below)
Mike Powell/Getty 44
Millbrook back flap (centre), 158–159
The Millton Vineyard 202, 203 (top)
Nautilus Estate of Marlborough 204
Neudorf Vineyards 206, 207 (top)
New Zealand Tourism Board back cover (art pieces, mussels, skiing), back flap (suite), 15 (top), 17 (top), 18 (top), 21 (below), 22, 27 (left), 28, 30, 31, 32, 34 (top), 36 (top left), 45, 48, 49, 51 (below), 52, 54, 55, 57, 63, 64, 66, 68 (top), 70, 114, 116 (top), 120, 122 (below), 126 (right), 129, 177, 179 (below), 180, 182 (right)
Nicara Lakeside Lodge 88–89
Owen Franken/Corbis 184 (below)
Paihia Beach Resort + Spa 90–91
Palliser Estate Wines of Martinborough 208
Panoramic Images/Getty 34 (below), 119
Paul Kennedy/Getty 60, 69
Paul Nevin/Photolibrary 13
Paul Souders/Corbis 24
Paul Thompson/Photolibrary 125
Paul Trummer/Getty 8
Pegasus Bay Winery 182 (left), 183, 184 (top), 210, 211 (below left)
Peppers Martinborough Hotel 92–93
Peppers on the Point 94–95

Pescatore Restaurant 211 (top; right centre)
Pete Seawards/Getty 5
Peter Adams/Getty 37
Peter Bush 18 (below), 68, 71, 113, 128
Peter Hendrie/Getty 117
The Postmaster's House Restaurant 195 (top right; centre)
Robert Dowling/Corbis 23 (top)
Robert Francis/Photolibrary 20
Roger Antrolous/Getty 124
Ron Redfern 65
Ross Land/Getty 25 (below),
Salute Restaurant 190 (right centre; below left)
Science Photo Library/Photolibrary front cover (volcano), 58, 67
Sharon Green/Photolibrary front cover (yacht), 26
Sherwood Lodge back cover (top centre), 160–161
SKYCITY Grand Hotel front cover (below right), 96–97
Solitaire Lodge 98–99
The Spire Queenstown 162–163
Steve Vidler/Photolibrary back cover (jetboat), 33 (below left), 126 (top)
Takaro 164–165
Terrôir Restaurant 192 (top right), 193
Thomas Barwick/Getty 181
Thomas Wester/Photolibrary 19
Treetops Lodge + Wilderness Estate 100–101
Uli Wiesmeier/Corbis front cover (rock), 118
The Villa Book 104–107, 168–171
Villa Maria Estate 212–213
Waipoua Lodge 102–103
The Wharf Café, Bar + Restaurant 203 (below right)
White Restaurant at Hilton Auckland 215
Wilfried Krecichwost/Getty 16

The publishers would like to thank the New Zealand Tourism Board and Karen Walker for their help and support during the production of this book.

Accolades Boutique Hotel (page 74)
31 Flemington Place, Brunswick Park, RD 4, Rotorua 3074
telephone : +64.7.345 5033
facsimile : +64.7.345 5066
email : stay@accolades.co.nz
website : www.accolades.co.nz

Air New Zealand (page 216)
UK reservations : 0800 028 4149 (24 hrs)
website : www.airnewzealand.co.uk

Antipodes Water (page 214)
421 St Lukes, PO Box 41, Auckland 1346
telephone : +64.9.846 9651
facsimile : +64.9.846 9650
email : info@antipodes.co.nz
website : www.antipodes.co.nz

Antoine's Restaurant (page 204)
333 Parnell Road, PO Box 37395, Parnell, Auckland 1001
telephone : +64.9.379 8756
facsimile : +64.9.524 0684
email : antoines@xtra.co.nz
website : www.antoinesrestaurant.co.nz/restaurant.html

Ata Rangi (page 190)
Puruatanga Road, PO Box 43, Martinborough 5741
telephone : +64.3.306 9570
facsimile : +64.3.306 9523
email : wines@atarangi.co.nz
website : www.atarangi.co.nz

Blanket Bay (page 138)
PO Box 35 Glenorchy, Otago 9350
telephone : +64.3.441 0115
facsimile : +64.3.442 9441
email : information@blanketbay.com
website : www.blanketbay.com

The Boatshed (page 76)
Crn Tawa and Huia Street, Little Oneroa, Waiheke 1081, Hauraki Gulf
telephone : +64.9.372 3242
facsimile : +64.9.372 3262
email : enquiries@boatshed.co.nz
website : www.boatshed.co.nz

Boulcott Street Bistro (page 208)
99 Boulcott Street, Wellington 6011
telephone : +64.4.499 4199
facsimile : +64.4.499 3879
email : info@boulcottsbistro.co.nz
website : www.boulcottstreetbistro.co.nz

Browns Sotheby's International Realty (page 166)
Russell Reddell, International Business Development, Ground Floor, Sofitel, 8 Duke Street, Queenstown 9300
telephone : +64.3.450 0483
facsimile : +64.3.450 0484
email : russell.reddell@sothebysrealty.com
website : www.brownssothebysrealty.com

Cardrona Terrace Estate (page 140)
84 Morris Road, RD 2, Wanaka 9382
telephone : +64.3.443 8020
facsimile : +64.3.443 1137
email : info@cardronaterrace.com
website : www.cardronaterrace.com

The Castle Matakana (page 78)
378 Whitmore Road, Matakana, RD 6, Warkworth, Rodney District, Auckland 0986
telephone : +64.9.422 9288
facsimile : +64.9.422 9289
email : mail@the-castle.co.nz
website : www.the-castle.co.nz

Cibo Restaurant (page 212)
91 St Georges Bay Road, PO Box 37234, Parnell, Auckland
telephone : +64.9.303 9660
facsimile : +64.9.303 9661
email : enquiry@cibo.co.nz
website : www.cibo.co.nz

Claremont Country Estate (page 142)
828 Ram Paddock Road, Waipara Gorge, RD 2, Amberley 7482, North Canterbury
telephone : +64.3.314 7559
facsimile : +64.3.314 7065
email : relax@claremont-estate.com
website : www.claremont-estate.com

Clearwater Cruises (page 108)
537 Spencer Road, RD 5, Lake Tarawera, Rotorua 3076
telephone : +64.7.362 8590
facsimile : +64.7.362 8591
email : cruise@clearwater.co.nz
website : www.clearwater.co.nz

Craggy Range Winery (page 192)
253 Waimarama Road, Havelock North, Hawkes Bay 4230
telephone : +64.6.873 7126
facsimile : +64.6.873 7141
email : info@craggyrange.com
website : www.craggyrange.com

Delamore Lodge (page 80)
83 Delamore Drive, PO Box 572, Waiheke Island 1041
telephone : +64.9.372 7372
facsimile : +64.9.372 7382
email : reservations@delamorelodge.com
website : www.delamorelodge.com

Eichardt's Private Hotel (page 144)
Marine Parade, Queenstown 9348
telephone : +64.3.441 0450
facsimile : +64.3.441 0440
email : stay@eichardtshotel.co.nz
website : www.eichardts.co.nz

directory

The Family of Twelve (page 188)
email : familyofXII@xtra.co.nz
website : www.familyoftwelve.co.nz

Felton Road (page 194)
Bannockburn, RD 2, Central Otago 9384
telephone : +64.3.445 0885
facsimile : +64.3.445 0881
email : wines@feltonroad.com
website : www.feltonroad.com

The French Café (page 198)
210 Symonds Street, Auckland 1010
telephone : +64.9.377 1911
website : www.thefrenchcafe.co.nz

Fromm Winery La Strada (page 196)
Godfrey Road, RD 2, Blenheim 7272, Marlborough
telephone : +64.3.572 9355
facsimile : +64.3.572 9366
email : lastrada@frommwineries.com
website : www.frommwineries.com

Gibb's Vineyard Restaurant (page 197)
258 Jacksons Road, RD 3, Blenheim 7273, Marlborough
telephone : +64.3.572 8048
facsimile : +64.3.572 8048
email : info@gibbs-restaurant.co.nz
website : www.gibbs-restaurant.co.nz

Glacier Southern Lakes Helicopters (page 172)
2 Lucas Place, PO Box 2152, Queenstown 9349
telephone : +64.3.442 3016
facsimile : +64.3.442 3019
email : qtown@glaciersouthernlakes.co.nz
website : www.glaciersouthernlakes.co.nz

Hapuku Lodge (page 146)
State Highway 1, Station Road, RD 1, Kaikoura 7371
telephone : +64.3.319 6559
facsimile : +64.3.319 6557
email : info@hapukulodge.com
website : www.hapukulodge.com

HELiPRO (page 108)
Hemo Road, PO Box 291, Te-Puia, Rotorua 3201
telephone : +64.7.357 2512
facsimile : +64.7.357 2502
email : rotorua@helipro.co.nz
website : www.helipro.co.nz

Heritage Hotel + Spa du Vin (page 82)
Lyons Road, Mangatawhiri Valley, RD 1, Pokeno 2471
telephone : +64.9.233 6314
facsimile : +64.9.233 6215
email : res@heritagehotels.co.nz
website : www.heritagehotels.co.nz

Herzog Luxury Restaurant (page 200)
81 Jeffries Rd, RD 3, Blenheim 7273
telephone : +64.3.572 8770
facsimile : +64.3.572 8730
email : info@herzog.co.nz
website : www.herzog.co.nz

Hopgood's Restaurant + Bar (page 206)
284 Trafalgar Street, Nelson 7010
telephone : +64.3.545 7191
fascimile : +64.3.545 7151
email : hopgoods@xtra.co.nz

Hotel Off The Square (page 148)
115 Worcester Street, Christchurch 0800
telephone : +64.3.374 9980
facsimile : +64.3.374 9987
email : enquiries@offthesquare.co.nz
website : www.offthesquare.co.nz

Huka Lodge (page 84)
Huka Falls Road, PO Box 95, Taupo 3351
telephone : +64.7.378 5791
facsimile : +64.7.378 0427
email : reservations@hukalodge.co.nz
website : www.hukalodge.com

Huntley House (page 150)
67 Yaldhurst Road, Upper Riccarton,
Christchurch 8042
telephone : +64.3.348 8435
facsimile : +64.3.341 6833
email : reservations@huntleyhouse.co.nz
website : www.huntleyhouse.co.nz

Kincaid Lodge (page 152)
611 Main North Road, RD 1, Kaikoura 7371
telephone : +64.3.319 6851
facsimile : +64.3.319 6801
email : helen@kincaidlodge.co.nz
website : www.kincaidlodge.co.nz

Kumeu River Wines (page 198)
550 State Highway 16, PO Box 24,
Kumeu 0841
telephone : +64.9.412 8415
facsimile : +64.9.412 7627
email : enquiries@kumeuriver.co.nz
website : www.kumeuriver.co.nz

Lawson's Dry Hills (page 200)
Alabama Road, PO Box 4020, Redwood Village,
Blenheim 7242
telephone : +64.3.578 7674
facsimile : +64.3.578 7603
email : wine@lawsonsdryhills.co.nz
website : www.lawsonsdryhills.co.nz

Lodge at 199 (page 86)
199 Spencer Road, Lake Tarawera, Rotorua 3076
telephone : +64.7.362 8122
fascimile : +64.7.362 8255
email : lodge@199.co.nz
website : www.199.co.nz

The Lodge at Paratiho Farms (page 154)
545 Waiwhero Road, RD 2, Upper Moutere,
Nelson 7175
telephone : +64.3.528 2100
facsimile : +64.3.528 2101
email : lodge@paratiho.co.nz
website : www.paratiho.co.nz

Matakauri Lodge (page 156)
Glenorchy Road, PO Box 888, Queenstown 7467
telephone : +64.3.441 1008
facsimile : +64.3.441 2180
email : relax@matakauri.co.nz
website : www.matakauri.co.nz

Millbrook (page 158)
Malaghans Road, Arrowtown, Queenstown 9371
telephone : +64.3.441 7000
facsimile : +64.3.441 7007
email : reservations@millbrook.co.nz
website : www.millbrook.co.nz

The Millton Vineyard (page 202)
CMB 66, Manutuke, Gisborne 4053
telephone : +64.6.862 8680
facsimile : +64.6.862 8869
email : inspired@millton.co.nz
website : www.millton.co.nz

Nautilus Estate of Marlborough (page 204)
12 Rapaura Road, Renwick,
Marlborough 7243
telephone : +64.3.572 9364
facsimile : +64.3.572 9374
email : sales@nautilusestate.com
website : www.nautilusestate.com

Navigate Oceania
Karine Thomas, 'Posada' building, 5/340 Parnell Road,
Auckland 1052
telephone : +64.9.307 3633
facsimile : +64.9.307 3292
email : info@navigateoceania.com
website : www.navigateoceania.com

Neudorf Vineyards (page 206)
Neudorf Road, Upper Moutere, Nelson 7175
telephone : +64.3.543 2643
facsimile : +64.3.543 2955
email : wine@neudorf.co.nz
website : www.neudorf.co.nz

Nicara Lakeside Lodge (page 88)
30–32 Ranginui Street, Ngongotaha, Rotorua 3010
telephone : +64.7.357 2105
facsimile : +64.7.357 5385
email : info@nicaralodge.co.nz
website : www.nicaralodge.co.nz

Paihia Beach Resort + Spa (page 90)
116 Marsden Road, PO Box 180, Paihia, Bay of Islands 0247
telephone : +64.9.402 0111
facsimile : +64.9.402 6026
email : info@paihiabeach.co.nz
website : www.paihiabeach.co.nz

Palliser Estate Wines of Martinborough (page 208)
PO Box 121, Kitchener St, Martinborough 5741
telephone : +64.6.306 9019
facsimile : +64.6.306 9946
email : palliser@palliser.co.nz
website : www.palliser.co.nz

Pegasus Bay Winery (page 210)
263 Stockgrove Road, RD 2, Amberley 7482, North Canterbury
telephone : +64.3.314 6869
facsimile : +64.3.314 6861
email : info@pegasusbay.com
website : www.pegasusbay.com

Peppers Martinborough Hotel (page 92)
The Square, Martinborough 5711
telephone : +64.6.306 9350
facsimile : +64.6.306 9345
email : martinborough@peppers.co.nz
website : www.martinboroughhotel.co.nz

Peppers on the Point (page 94)
214 Kawaha Point Road, Rotorua 3010
telephone : +64.7.348 4868
facsimile : +64.7.348 1868
email : onthepoint@peppers.co.nz
website : www.peppers.co.nz/on-the-point

Pescatore Restaurant (page 210)
The George Hotel, 50 Park Terrace, Canterbury 8001
telephone : +64.3.371 0257
facsimile : +64.3.366 6747
email : fandb@thegeorge.com
website : www.thegeorge.com

The Postmaster's House Restaurant (page 194)
54 Buckingham Street, Arrowtown, Central Otago 9302
telephone : +64.3.442 0991
facsimile : +64.3.442 0983
email : bookings@postmastershouse.com
website : www.postmastershouse.com

Saluté Restaurant (page 190)
83 Main Street, Greytown 5953
telephone : +64.6.304 9825
facsimile : +64.6.304 9829
email : reservations@salute.greytown.co.nz
website : www.salute.greytown.co.nz

Sherwood Lodge (page 160)
919 Sherwood Road, RD 1, Waiau, North Canterbury 8275
telephone : +64.3.315 6078
facsimile : +64.3.315 6424
email : sherwoodlodge@xtra.co.nz
website : www.sherwoodlodge.co.nz

SKYCITY Grand Hotel (page 96)
90 Federal Street, PO Box 90643, Auckland 1010
telephone : +64.9.363 7000
facsimile : +64.9.363 7010
email : reservations@skycitygrand.co.nz
website : www.skycitygrand.co.nz

Solitaire Lodge (page 98)
Lake Tarawera, RD 5, Rotorua 3076
telephone : +64.7.362 8208
facsimile : +64.7.362 8445
email : solitaire@solitairelodge.co.nz
website : www.solitairelodge.com

The Spire Queenstown (page 162)
3–5 Church Lane, PO Box 1129,
Queenstown 9300
telephone : +64.3.441 0004
facsimile : +64.3.441 0003
email : queenstown@thespirehotels.com
website : www.thespirehotels.com

Takaro (page 164)
914 Takaro Road, Te Anau 9640
telephone : +64.3.249 0161
facsimile : +64.3.249 0111
email : contact@takarolodge.com
website : www.takarolodge.com

Terrôir Restaurant (page 192)
253 Waimarama Road, Havelock North,
Hawkes Bay 4230
telephone : +64.6.873 0143
email : info@craggyrange.com
website : www.craggyrange.com

Treetops Lodge + Wilderness Estate (page 100)
351 Kearoa Road, RD 1, Horohoro,
Rotorua 3077
telephone : +64.7.333 2066
facsimile : +64.7.333 2065
email : info@treetops.co.nz
website : www.treetops.co.nz

The Villa Book (pages 104, 168)
12 Venetian House, 47 Warrington Crescent,
London W9 1EJ
telephone : +44.845.500 2000
facsimile : +44.845.500 2001
email : info@thevillabook.com
website : www.thevillabook.com

Villa Maria Estate (page 212)
118 Montgomerie Road, PO Box 43046, Mangere,
Auckland
telephone : +64.9.255 0660
facsimile : +64.9.255 0661
email : enquiries@villamaria.co.nz
website : www.villamaria.co.nz

Waipoua Lodge (page 102)
State Highway 12, RD 6, Dargaville 0376, Northland
telephone : +64.9.439 0422
facsimile : +64.9.523 8081
email : nicole@waipoualodge.co.nz
website : www.waipoualodge.co.nz

The Wharf Café, Bar + Restaurant (page 202)
60 The Esplanade, Gisborne 4010
telephone : +64.6.868 4876
facsimile : +64.6.868 4876
email : lew@wharfbar.co.nz
website : www.wharfbar.co.nz

White Restaurant at Hilton Auckland (page 214)
Prince Wharf, 147 Quay Street,
Auckland 1010
telephone : +64.9.978 2020
facsimile : +64.9.978 2001
email : team@whiterestaurant.co.nz
website : www.whiterestaurant.co.nz